The Ice Cave

The Ice Cave

A Woman's Adventures from the Mojave to the Antarctic

Lucy Jane Bledsoe

Terrace Books
A trade imprint of the University of Wisconsin Press

Terrace Books
A trade imprint of the University of Wisconsin Press
1930 Monroe Street
Madison, Wisconsin 53711

3 Henrietta Street
London WC2E 8LU, England

Printed in the United States of America

ISBN 978-0-7394-7392-4

Contents

Acknowledgments

I have had the extraordinary good fortune to travel twice to Antarctica as a guest of the National Science Foundation. The stupendous Artists and Writers in Antarctica program, which fosters dialogue between scientists and artists, was administered for many years by Guy Guthridge; without his vision and good will, this book never could have happened. Many scientists on the Ice shared their camps and gave generously of their time and knowledge. I particularly want to thank Dr. David Ainley, Dr. Nils Halverson, Michelle Hester, Dr. Berry Lyons, Dr. Dave Marchant, Hanna Nevins, Michael Solarz, and Dr. Brian Stewart. I couldn't have made the second trip without Elaine Hood's invaluable logistical support. Ted Dettmar, Robbie Score, Rae Spain, and Commander Stephen M. Wheeler of the U.S. Coast Guard all offered needed guidance. So many other people at all three American stations—McMurdo, Amundsen-Scott South Pole, and Palmer—also provided generous support. For help in getting me to Antarctica in the first place, I want to thank Karen Baker, Linnea Due, Jane Fisher, Regina Griffin, Sheri Krams, Frank Lucian, Olivia Martinez, and Craig Southard. I also want to thank Peregrine Adventures for taking me onboard the Russian ship, the *Akademik Sergey Vavilov,* for my third trip to Antarctica.

The California Arts Council provided me with a fellowship at a crucial time in the development of this project, and I am very grateful not only for the personal support but also for the heroic efforts of that organization to keep the arts alive and funded in California.

For sharing trails and waterways with me, big thank yous to Anne Binninger, Suzanne Case, Wendy Eliot, Katie Deamer, Peggy Deamer, Kendal Hansen, Vivian Kleiman, Robbie Liben, Peggy Malloy, Priscilla McKenney, Georgena Moran, Beth Parazette, Sarah Purdy, Shannon Smith, Karen Tredick, and Mary Wildeman. I am grateful to John and Helen Bledsoe for taking me on my first hiking trips and canoe paddles. These journeys are the heart of my work.

For reading these pages and offering their insights, I am indebted to Linnea Due, Martha Garcia, Kanani Kauka, Susan Fox Rogers, and Barbara Sjoholm. Two anonymous reviewers for the University of Wisconsin Press offered particularly useful feedback that guided the last revision of the book. Thank you to the wonderful staff at the University of Wisconsin Press, including Carla Aspelmeier, Andrea Christofferson, Benson Gardner, Maggie Hilliard, and Adam Mehring.

Finally, I want to thank Alison Bechdel for ongoing dialogue that has helped me deepen my understanding of the relationship between creativity and will; Cheryl Jones for hearing my stories of fear and grace better than anyone; and Raphael Kadushin of the University of Wisconsin Press for believing in this project. Pat Mullan has been my favorite companion on all the journeys.

Earlier versions of the following essays, or excerpts thereof, have been previously published: "The Freedom Machine" in *Bicycling* and *WIG Magazine;* "On Being at Sea" in *Women on the Verge,* edited by Susan Fox Rogers, and *The Unsavvy Traveler,* edited by Rosemary Caperton, Anne Mathews, and Lucie Ocenas; "Above Treeline" in *Solo: On Her Own Adventure,* edited by Susan Fox Rogers;

"Reconnaissance" in *Hot Ticket,* edited by Linnea Due; "How to Prey" in *Eastbay Express.* Much of the history of cycling information in "The Freedom Machine" comes from an essay by Lisa Larrabee, "Women and Cycling: The Early Years," which accompanies a reprint of Frances E. Willard's book, *How I Learned to Ride the Bicycle* (Sunnyvale, CA: Fair Oaks Publishing Company, 1991). For this book, some names have been changed and places disguised to protect the privacy of the individuals described herein.

The Ice Cave

Prologue
Hope Valley

I was three years old and camping in Oregon's Mount Jefferson Wilderness with my large family and our friends. I don't remember toddling away from camp, but I do remember the luminescent ice cave and my sense of extraordinary wonder as I crawled into its deepest recess where the translucent blue encompassed me. The cave's interior had slowly melted out over the summer, forming ridges and dips in its walls, like the crests and troughs of waves. The chilled air bathed my cheeks and the meltwater on the cave's floor soaked into my corduroy pants. I remember feeling utterly content.

My serenity was ruined by the appearance of several agitated adult faces at the mouth of the ice cave. I was shocked that they considered me lost, and now found, but I didn't have the vocabulary to express my confusion. Someone, probably my father, dropped to all fours and gingerly crawled in to get me out of that, apparently, very dangerous place. Though I'm sure I didn't have cogent, well-formed thoughts about my predicament, somewhere in my developing mind and heart I did know that their place of danger felt like my haven.

This is my earliest memory of finding a spiritual habitat in the wilderness.

As a child, I canoed the rivers and hiked the trails of the Pacific Northwest with my family. I'll never forget my first pack, a child-size Trapper Nelson. This torture device had one big sack made of tan, heavy-duty canvas and two perfectly straight wooden stakes, the ends of which rested on the packer's hips. I can still picture perfectly the two huge, purple bruises on my mother's hips from carrying her adult-size Trapper Nelson.

There were times on these family outings when I resented the strenuousness of our activities, when I felt hungry and cold. And yet, when the rest of my family outgrew the outdoor adventures, I began seeking the wilderness on my own. I joined a church youth group for a while because it organized mountain climbs and backpack trips, but that ended when I argued with a church youth leader about the veracity of evolution. I didn't understand then, at the age of twelve, as I don't understand now, how anyone could ever believe that science conflicts with spirituality. Science is a deep exploration and understanding of the complete miracle of our universe. The people from that church didn't agree, though, so after leaving it behind I sought and found other wilderness trips through organizations like the Oregon Museum of Science and Industry and the American Heritage Society. Somehow, I managed to find people with whom to bicycle the Oregon coast and hike the Pacific Crest Trail, until I reached the age at which I could hike, bike, and ski on my own.

For many years, these forays into the forests, deserts, rivers, and mountains provided me with solace. I have always felt untethered, as if I were born wild and without a home. I assumed from a very young age that I would need to learn to survive on my own, and each trip into the wilderness was proof that I needed nothing and nobody, that breathing mountain air and walking alpine trails fulfilled me. The tremendous longing that always has accompanied me dissipated in the mountains and I found relief, a kind of peace. My whole life I have searched for that ice cave or its equivalent in a mountain pass or a desert night, and I often have found it, moments of grace in the wilderness.

A few years ago, my wilderness trips began, occasionally, to fail me. I don't mean that I didn't make the summit or complete a route; I mean that the wilderness didn't transform me, didn't clear out my loneliness, didn't put my life in perspective. Somehow, it was no longer enough to prove to myself that I had all the skills I needed to survive, anywhere and anytime. These trips in which I failed to find solace became more and more frequent. I had begun to feel more frightened of life and less connected to anything authentic. I felt that my achievements had been accomplished through a force of will, that determination was all that kept me going.

So, four days before Christmas, a time when even the diehard wilderness travelers were shopping, I drove up to the Sierras and parked my car in the lot at the foot of Hope Valley. A quick overnight, I promised myself. A little shot of serenity to get me through the rest of the holidays and to ward off the unhappy thoughts and feelings crowding me. I would straighten myself out with a couple days of backcountry skiing, a night alone in a tent, 360 degrees of mountains for twenty-four hours—a formula that used to work without fail. It would work this time, I told myself. It *had* to work. I would make it work. If I just tried harder, I could rediscover grace.

On my drive up to the mountains I stopped at the ranger station to check on the weather. A ranger confirmed what I already had learned on the Internet: a storm hovered far offshore in the Pacific, would probably head north and miss California altogether, and in any case wouldn't hit land for three days. No problem, I would be out by tomorrow afternoon.

I began skiing across the meadow in Hope Valley, feeling depressed by the gray tableau. The sky looked blank, colorless, and the trees were a gunmetal green, rigid and dark. I pushed on, knowing that about six miles ahead was a rise where the trees thinned and opened onto a view of mountains. I was determined to reach that place to make my camp. I needed a view. I changed from my dark glasses to my regular ones, ignoring the icy air laden with crackling negative ions, and skied on. And on and on and on.

The time passed easily, though I never broke through to an easy place in my mind. I worried about work, friends, and family, but not about the sky that was turning a darker and more ominous gray. By the time I reached the rise where I wanted to camp, the clouds had socked in so thickly there was no view anyway. It began to snow lightly as I pitched my tent. I cooked a quick supper of ramen and, *still* ignoring the impending storm, snapped into my skis for a quick prebed jaunt. I slid down to frozen Burnside Lake, looked around, and skied back up the hill. By now a steely wind blew the snow at a forty-five degree angle, and I decided to tie the tent down with guy lines. By the time I crawled in, it was snowing hard.

I lay awake all night in one of those high-altitude stupors, having no real thoughts but feeling no relaxation either. I read a book and then lay there listening to the silence. Eventually, the wind died completely and I looked forward to skiing out in the morning. The dusting of snow that had fallen in the evening would make the downhill ski fast and maybe even fun.

When a faint, early daylight finally brightened the ceiling of my tent, I sat up ready to go and didn't care if I would be at my car by eight in the morning, home by noon. I wanted out of there, away from this landscape that once delighted me but now only served as a constant reinforcement of how bleak I felt.

I unzipped the door and a pile of powdery snow cascaded into my tent, burying my book, knees, and hands. I pulled on my waterproof pants and jacket and pushed my way through the drift. But it wasn't a drift. It was the actual snow depth: to my complete astonishment, four feet had fallen in the night. And was still falling. The storm that was due in three days, the storm that was supposed to have whooshed north to Oregon, had arrived here and now in California.

I knew that I needed a hot meal. I also knew that, given the weather, I should stay put. But I could also tell by the lazy drift of the falling snow, the solid gray of the sky, that this storm had a few days in her, that it was either get out now or spend several nights, including Christmas Eve and Day, in this tent. I cooked some hot cereal, dug out my tent, and packed up.

The snow was far too dry and powdery to ski on top of, so I had to push through the thigh-high stuff. For six miles. For six hours.

Though the route should have been a simple one, a forest service road through the trees, in the storm it was often difficult to tell which opening in the trees was the road. Sometimes visibility was only a few feet. I could have easily veered off into the forest and become lost. Yet I pushed forward, shoving rather than skiing, through the deep snow.

I had never been so physically exhausted in my life. My thinking felt sluggish, but I kept reminding myself of options, that at any time I could pitch the tent again (in what? this powder?) and crawl into my sleeping bag to wait out the storm. But I wanted so badly to go home that I plowed, quite literally, forward. I did stop once under a tree so big and densely branched that it blocked the falling snow, making a place where I could actually feel solid earth beneath me. Without taking off my skis, I pulled out my stove and made hot soup. I had no appetite, but I knew that hunger was making me even more stupid. I force fed myself the soup and a Powerbar. Chewing and swallowing felt like a workout.

Eventually, I reached the place where the road dove steeply down into a meadow. Only about two hundred yards across that meadow was my car. Even so, it was at this juncture that I became truly frightened. I could see nothing. It was a total whiteout by now. As I entered the meadow, I no longer had the dark corridor of trees on either side of me to use as guides, and I knew that it would be easy to wander around directionless for hours. I remembered a stream that ran through the meadow and actually found the indent of its path. But following it proved impossible. The streambed made irregularities in the snow depth and I kept falling down, sinking into the stuff up to my neck. Getting up from a bed of deep powder, with a pack on my back and long skis on my feet, was grueling. I was afraid that the time would come when I would not be able to get up, so I headed away from the stream. I couldn't even stay to the side of it, use it as a direction guide, because I couldn't see the stream unless I was in it.

A yellow smudge looming in the storm ahead presented itself as a sign of hope. I knew what it was: the *Stop Ahead* sign at the edge of the parking lot. I was just yards from my car now, but my energy was running out. I felt as if I were in the classic wilderness fuck-up scenario: Didn't people always die just yards from their cabin or the highway?

I pushed on, made it to the yellow sign, and then beyond to my car, only to realize what I should have figured out a long time back: that the car was no haven whatsoever. It was a big white mound, entirely covered with the snow that would have insulated its interior somewhat, but not much because the car itself was made of conductive steel. My tent would be warmer than the car. But I wasn't about to set up my tent there in the meadow next to my car, a few yards from the highway. And of course the parking lot was entirely snowed in, so there was no possibility of driving away even if I could dig out my car.

Just then a great orange hulk, like Bigfoot himself, crept stealthily into my line of vision. It was the snowplow on the highway. I couldn't get there in time to intercept the driver, but if the road was plowed, surely I could walk on it to the nearby resort called Sorensen's.

The final obstacle between me and the highway was the worst one yet. The snowplow had created a giant berm, a pile of snow well over my own height, between the road and the parking lot. I had to reach down through the four-foot-deep snow to my feet in order to undo each ski, wrestle it to the surface, and then throw it like a spear over the berm and onto the highway. Getting my body over the berm proved even harder. The snow was still too soft to climb over, and yet it had solidified enough to make pushing *through* it very difficult as well. I fought the abominable snow berm unsuccessfully for a while. My strength was all but spent and I was forced to take rests, lying face down in the stuff and thinking how simple dying would be. I'd probably lose consciousness pretty quickly and would suffer nothing. If I lived alone in this world, I might have chosen that journey instead of the other one, the fighting through the damn berm journey. But I couldn't die now, couldn't do that to the people who loved me, so I took off my pack and unstrapped my snow shovel. By using a combination of shoveling, flailing, swimming, and kicking, all the while dragging my pack along with me, I eventually landed on the plowed highway.

To my amazement, just a few yards down the road at an intersection sat a highway patrol vehicle with an officer at the wheel. I stumbled toward him and dumped my pack beside the road. The officer opened the passenger door and told me to get in. I was soaked by then and began shaking so hard I couldn't speak. He tried to get me to drink what coffee was left in his Styrofoam cup, apologizing for it no longer being hot, but I couldn't use my hands at all for a while. Finally, I was able to ask if he could take me down the road to

Sorensen's Resort, but he said that he couldn't leave his post. His job was to block traffic from going up to Carson Pass where avalanches were sliding onto the highway. So I sat with him and waited for the snowplow to return. The officer warned me that the snowplow driver might have regulations against taking passengers but I planned on begging. In the meantime, the officer gave me a few safety tips, including suggesting that I carry a cell phone when I go out by myself.

The snowplow driver had a heart, broke regulations, and took me up the road to Sorensen's. I later learned that a whole crowd watched from the windows of the café as I disembarked from the monster machine, but at the time I knew only that I wanted warmth and a telephone. The owners of the resort were kind. They fixed me a hot chocolate, piled high with whipped cream, and sat me next to the fire in the café. I waited there in a stupor for several hours until they found a vacant cabin for me. After a hot bath I called home and then got under the covers. I lay there deeply appreciating the whole concept of bed—off the ground, foot-thick mattress, cotton sheets, down comforter—until I heard footsteps on my cabin's porch. When I got up and opened the door, I found a handwritten note from a couple in a nearby cabin inviting me to dinner. Wanting human contact, I dressed in my still soggy fleece pants and slogged over to their cabin.

The middle-aged newlyweds primarily wanted an audience for their born-again romance, and for a while I was willing to be that audience as they fed me hot buttered rum, roast beef, mashed potatoes, and hot blackberry pie. She had written a book on keeping romance alive, and they both told me about the many techniques she had devised. On this romantic weekend, for example, she had brought a package of strawberry Kool-Aid and had used it to make a big red heart in the snow outside their cabin. They told how they celebrate every week of their marriage with a letter of the alphabet.

The first week was the letter A, which meant that they gave one another apple candy, used the word "adore," wrote anthems about their love, bought one another sexy apparel. The husband gave me a conspiratorial smile and told me they were at the letter F this weekend. I thanked them and left shortly after dinner.

I was stuck at Sorensen's Resort for several days. I kept waiting for the release, not just from the storm outside but from the feeling of trudging through deep snow. It never came. I never felt that euphoria of having made it, of having survived a brush with danger, of being charged with a bright new aliveness, a feeling I had had many times in the past. Though I knew that I was the one who had made the mistakes, and also knew exactly what they were, I still felt betrayed. I had come to the wilderness for solace, for relief from the force of my own will, from the tedium of myself, and I had only found that force and tedium mirrored back at me. The six-hour blunder through the white tableau, the exhaustion, the fear, the uselessness of it all, did not carry me through to something new or enlightening. I couldn't shake the feeling of despair. The wilderness did not feel like my home anymore.

That botched winter journey triggered a long personal investigation into the meaning of my relationship with wilderness; the way I had been, my whole life, searching for home in the wild; and how I had come to this impasse between my spirit, the creative part of myself I liked best, and my ironclad will, a part that used to serve me well but had become a hindrance. I quickly saw that neither grace nor will could be understood without looking deeply at fear, a theme that had arisen time and again in my writings about the wild.

The following true stories explore different faces of this relationship between fear and grace, through many extraordinary journeys, leading eventually to the wildest, most remote earthly destination of all, Antarctica, where earlier explorers bashed themselves up against their own wills, and by example, helped to show me a different way.

I have come to think of wilderness as Earth's imagination, the regions that people have not organized for their own use. Language is another kind of wilderness: a rich, sprawling, biodiverse tangle through which we create paths, known as stories. This book is my own narrative path, chronicling my geographical journeys, in search of the twin wild cards, fear and grace. The stories in this book do not follow an arrow-like trajectory, shot from a place of fear to one of grace. The relationship between the two is cyclical, and at least for me, always will be. Imagination, adventure, and story are the rewards along the way.

The Freedom Machine

If I am asked to explain why I learned the bicycle, I should say I did it as an act of grace, if not actual religion.
Frances E. Willard, *How I Learned to Ride the Bicycle: Reflections of an Influential Nineteenth-century Woman*

My hiking partner and I were doing some high-speed desert driving, me riding shotgun with my bare feet up on the dash, on our way to a backpacking trailhead in the Rockies. We had promised ourselves that we would enter the Mojave in the early morning, even before dawn, but delays in packing put us on the road about ten in the morning. As we drove the endless midday miles with the windows down, breathing the lung-scorching air, I decided I liked the desert at high noon. I loved feeling stunned by its dragon's breath and lulled by the sight of its hallucinatory horizon.

"Can I turn on the air conditioning now?" Katie asked a little before noon.

"But don't you love the hot rush of air? The *real* air? How can we say we've experienced the desert if—"

"Okay, okay, okay."

Occasionally we passed an abandoned shack or trailer where someone had thought the cheap land worth a try at survival. I imagined their trips to Barstow for jugs of water, their afternoons—for surely they were unemployed to have chosen this for home—sitting limp in the thin wedges of shade cast by their shelters. I tried to guess how many days it took them to give up and quit. I admired these people who had tried this one last option, who had thought it might be better than urban homelessness, or moving back in with their folks, or even just better than a mortgage. Following my life-long habit of noting options, escape routes, lives I could live if I needed to live a different one, I put a mental Post-it on the Mojave Desert. I could live here if I had to. I could survive where others had not. I had skills.

At first I thought I was seeing a mirage: a shimmering on the highway ahead of us, sharp steely flashes of metal and the wavering image of a human. As we drew closer, I could have sworn it was a person on a bicycle, but it was high noon and we were eighty miles from the next town, a good twenty from the last one. It just didn't seem possible. Who would do such a thing? Then I laughed at myself: Most people's mirages are bodies of water; mine are of bicycles.

Ever since inheriting my sister's bicycle, an old, clunky yellow one-speed, I have been in love with two-wheelers. On my bike, I learned that landscape is a continuum, that the city rolls right into the mountains. I learned that my body knows secrets my head does not know, secrets that could be imagined into stories. On my bike, endorphins nourished my imagination.

Today, the shelves of my writing room hold bicycle models and the walls are covered with cycling posters. One of my favorite paintings is "Big Julie" by Fernand Léger, which portrays a large, jaunty woman holding a flower in one hand and a mangled bicycle in the other. Butterflies flutter between Julie and her bike. Some people have totem animals; I have a totem machine.

That I might hallucinate a woman on a bike in the desert made perfect sense, but as it turned out, this was no apparition. Before us was a real woman cycling across the Mojave Desert. We drew up behind the traveler and stared with disbelief at her long blond hair, the panniers on either side of her back wheel flapping open, revealing the clothing stuffed inside. Two smooth, varnished wooden sticks stuck out one of the panniers. She also had two Evian water bottles tied loosely to the stem of her saddle and they bonked against the panniers as she pedaled. The bike was a cheap-looking hybrid.

The only explanation I could think of was that this woman was doing a story for *Outside Magazine:* the Mojave Desert by bike, alone, in under eight hours. And for a moment I was overwhelmed with envy. I wanted out of our steel encasement. I wanted to feel the windblown sand in my face, the road grit under my tires. I wanted to taste the sage-flavored air, listen to the silence of the desert that is like no other silence. In other words, I wanted to move through this landscape slowly enough to engage all of my senses but fast enough to experience exhilaration, which meant I wanted to do it on a bicycle. But . . . not on a cheap one like this woman's. Not with water bottles dangling off the saddle. Up close I saw that she had anything but an athlete's body; she looked doughy. This cyclist moved too slowly, and too joylessly, to be an adventure tourist.

It took a few moments for Katie and me to come to terms with the fact that this cyclist was real, not a figment of the desert's imagination. Then it took us another moment to decide that we should check out whether or not she wanted to be alone with her bicycle in the Mojave at noon. By then we had shot past the woman, but Katie made a U-turn and headed back. We passed her again, made another U-turn, and then pulled alongside her.

I called out the passenger window, "Are you all right?"

She squinted at me.

"Need anything?"

"I could use a ride."

She definitely wasn't doing a story for *Outside Magazine.* Katie pulled over and I helped the woman unload her panniers. We threw those in the back seat and put her bicycle on top of our packs in the far back. Then she crawled in next to her panniers, and we got a better look at her. Her long blond hair was tangled and dirty. The skin on her face looked as if it had burnt and peeled a dozen times. She drained her water bottle, and we offered her water from our gallon jug. She refilled both of her Evian bottles, drank one down, and refilled it again, as if we might dump her back into the desert without notice. The only food we had in the car were Powerbars. She ate two in succession—a feat of true hunger—and took two more for later. We rolled up the windows and turned on the air conditioning. My playing at desert survival had lost its appeal.

Though Barbara told us her first name, she could not, or would not, tell us where she was going, so we rode in silence for a while, feeling nervous and awkward. I surreptitiously checked the location of my wallet. Was this some kind of scam? Had we fallen into the hands of a highway con artist? But the devoured Powerbars and her sunblistered face did not jibe with any possible scam I could think up.

Finally Katie and I began chatting to one another about our upcoming backpacking trip, trying to fill the awkward silence. Apparently our conversation eased her mind about us, and eventually she began asking questions about our trip. We in turn tried questioning her again and this time received answers. In fact, we learned a great deal about her life and the purpose of her Mojave crossing.

Barbara had been married for twenty years. Her husband had broken her arm twice, three ribs once, her jaw once, and left her body covered with bruises more times than she could remember. He had prohibited her from ever leaving the house. If she did, and he found out about it, she got a beating. He also prohibited her from earning any money of her own and from having friends. The couple had two sons, the second of which had left home a month before we met Barbara. She had been waiting for that leave-taking for most of the twenty years of her marriage. The same week her youngest son left, Barbara took his bicycle and panniers, which he had left in the garage, and made her escape one morning after her husband left for work.

Those first hours were the most terrifying, she told us. She took only back roads, which lessened his chance of finding her. But if he had found her, he would have had a lot of deserted, witness-free territory for the punishment he would have surely handed out. By back roads, it took her days just to get out of her home range. With each passing day she felt a little safer, though never completely safe.

Barbara hadn't the money to fly or to take a bus anywhere, but with the bicycle and enough cash to buy bread and peanut butter she was making her way to a small town on the other side of the Mojave, the home of a childhood friend with whom she had not been in touch for years. Because her husband had doggedly recorded the addresses and phone numbers of all of her acquaintances, she had had to choose a destination that had never crossed his path. This childhood friend did not know that Barbara was coming. In fact, Barbara had told no one of her plans, not even her mother or sister for fear that her husband would coerce them into giving him information, as he had done in the past.

By the time we met Barbara, she had cycled for twenty-four days and covered about six hundred miles. From the looks of her, the average of twenty-five miles a day would have been a full workout. She said that she usually slept in the heat of midday and rode mornings and early evenings. Occasionally she forked out the cash to stay at a campground for a shower, but most often slept in culverts. On the day we found her, she had begun to feel desperate. It was getting very hot and she had seen no culverts, no shade, no hiding places. It was as if she had been oblivious to the fact that the highway she was following had entered a desert.

As I stared out at the unending sand and sky and listened to Barbara, a new wave of envy blew through me. I thought it crude to envy a woman who was forced to escape an abusive relationship by means of a grueling physical journey. But she was, in fact, *making the journey.* She was running away. She was claiming her own path and doing it with a bicycle. I envied her for having the guts.

For all of my life, as far back as I can remember, I have longed to be somewhere else. Somewhere wilder. Somewhere warmer. Somewhere with more heart. As a child, I found temporary escape on my bicycle. Riding hard—until the sweat ran down my back, until my lungs felt like bursting—scoured out my confusion and pain, delivering me to a bright place of contentment. Today I still try to ride to that place. Getting on my bicycle is synonymous with saying, *I'm outta here.* If I'm lucky, ten or twenty miles into a ride, escape, wilderness, and freedom combust together and burn off my fear. I can, on my bicycle, arrive at places of great courage.

And yet, just as I play at desert survival with mind games in the car, or even during backpack trips of a few days duration, my escapes by bicycle have been child's play compared to Barbara's use of the freedom machine.

I tried to tell her how big her courage looked to me.

But she only shrugged and said that the bicycle ride across mountains and desert didn't scare her half as much as her marriage had. In fact, though she told stories of difficulties on the road, she preferred talking about her traveling triumphs. Her favorite story was about the time she was ascending a mountain pass and came to a sign announcing that the road from that point on was closed. Unable to imagine turning back, she continued forward until she came to the place where a road crew was clearing a huge rockslide. She hoisted her bicycle and carried it across the rubble to the amazement, and eventual admiration, of the road crew. They applauded her when she finally reached the other side of the long stretch of broken rock. About five times she told us about that applause, and I realize now that it must have sustained her across much more than the debris of one rockslide.

I have spent several years thinking about Barbara and her story. Her appearance in my life has felt mythic, a backward-and-forward-looking message that I couldn't decipher. Meeting Barbara in the wilderness of the Mojave struck a chord that sounded so loudly inside me that I couldn't find any context for her journey. But it did have a context, and as I reflected on it over time the historical one was the easiest place to start.

When the bicycle craze hit the United States at the end of the nineteenth century, women immediately saw this new machine as a vehicle of emancipation. In 1895, Frances Willard, the temperance leader and suffragette, wrote a book called *A Wheel within a Wheel* on how the bicycle and cycling serve as the perfect extended metaphor for the feminist cause, indeed for all things important in life, from health to politics. Willard grew up on the prairie and spent her childhood romping out-of-doors. She insisted on wearing her hair short, which was very unusual for a girl at that time, and on being called Frank. She wrote that she "ran wild" until her sixteenth birthday, at which time she was forced into long skirts, corsets, and high heels. Though she spent most of her adult life working for temperance and women's suffrage, she did not regain her personal freedom until 1893 when at the age of fifty-three she learned to ride a bicycle. Willard equated mastering the bicycle with controlling a woman's personal destiny, claiming her own path.

Susan B. Anthony agreed, saying that bicycling gave women "a feeling of freedom and self-reliance," and that a woman on a bicycle is "the picture of free, untrammeled womanhood." Anthony claimed that bicycling did "more to emancipate woman than anything else in the world."

As more and more women took to "the wheel," manufacturers began making bicycles and other cycling products especially for women. The Starley Brothers made the first mass-produced women's bike, the "Psycho Ladies' Bicycle," and other manufacturers came up with products to battle the prevalent idea that cycling ruined women's femininity. One company invented a screen that, once attached to the bicycle, shielded the view of a lady's ankles and feet.

Even with such precautions, female cyclists were scorned by the dominant media. The proliferation and vehemence of newspaper and magazine editorials blasting women cyclists proved that men were quite aware of the bicycle's role as an avenue to freedom. Some wrote that the freedom felt on a bicycle might intoxicate women to the point of wanting, perhaps even demanding, other freedoms. Others believed that the shape of a bicycle seat might stimulate a woman in immoral ways. Groups even lobbied to have bicycles outlawed for women. These pundits warned that, on a bicycle, a woman had no need for an escort. Though the logic of this fear is difficult to grasp—Did she not need an escort because she could now out-pedal dangerous encounters on her own?—it is easy to see how the idea of women not needing men would severely challenge the status quo. In 1895, in the *Minneapolis Tribune,* Ann Strong stated that bicycles were "just as good company as most husbands," and better yet, when you're tired of your bicycle, you can "dispose of it and get a new one without shocking the entire community." The Victorian Era, and many of its strict rules intended to protect women's femininity, was on its way out and some women were riding the bicycle to get away faster. In 1896, Margaret Valentine Le Long ignored her family and friends who begged her to stay home and rode her bicycle, alone, from Chicago to San Francisco. She wore a skirt and carried a pistol.

I wonder what Barbara of the Mojave would have to say about Willard's book and theses, about Anthony's declaration, about Le Long's armed trek across two-thirds of the continent. For Barbara, the bicycle meant freedom in its most literal form: physical survival. Perhaps the urgency of her journey was too great for her to have been able to reflect on her place in the history of women, bicycles, and freedom.

As it turned out, we had found Barbara on the last leg of her journey. The next town, or so she told us, was her destination. As we drew closer to the home of her childhood friend, her talk turned to her future. She thought her friend would welcome her, but for how long? She had to find work, which would be very difficult since she hadn't held a job in twenty years. She spoke with pride of the one-woman gardening business she had had before her marriage. Although most of her tools were long gone, she carried in her panniers a large pair of clipping shears, which she talked about almost as much as she talked about the road crew's applause. I imagined that that one pair of shears was her only reminder of her skills, of her independence, of her ability to take care of herself.

Barbara didn't know, or didn't want us to know, the exact location of her friend's house and told us to drop her off at a gas station in town. As we pulled off the highway to let her out, I imagined that it was me getting ready to begin a new life there. The air was dusty hot and the few buildings looked more like children's forts, boards nailed roughly together, than bona fide establishments. The homely starkness attracted me. Perhaps I could hide from other people here, but I could never hide from myself. Where could I go? One step out the door and it would be me, sand, and sky. Maybe the desert, even this weather-beaten town, wasn't the last resort I had assumed it to be. Maybe it was a first resort. Maybe it was the beginning.

"Will you be okay?" I asked Barbara, meaning, did she feel safe from her husband, and perhaps meaning, could she find her friend's house. She cast her eyes over the few businesses in that tiny dry town and said something about finding work. "A waitressing job, maybe," she said, "but without any experience . . ." It was as if we didn't even exist anymore. She had escaped her hometown, tackled the Sierras and the desert, and now she turned without pause to the next challenge. I guessed that she had had a lot of practice living life like a video game, clearing one obstacle and bracing herself, immediately, for the next one.

I told her that I hoped there would be some sensible employer in town who would realize that riding a bicycle six hundred miles over the Sierras and across the Mojave said a lot more about a person's character and capabilities than previous experience serving bacon and eggs. She smiled for the first time and said she hoped that was the case. We gave her the rest of our Powerbars and some cash.

As Katie and I drove away, we were silent for a few minutes, and then we admitted to one another that we were each trying to find flaws in Barbara's story, again wondering if she could have been some kind of highway con artist. But as hard as we tried, we could think of no way that a woman riding a bicycle alone across a desert could be a con. In fact, our searching for an explanation other than the one Barbara gave us was absurd. Domestic violence is as common as dirt. What is uncommon is Barbara's courage, her willingness to cross any physical landscape to overcome the interior landscape of her life. The truth is that when I met Barbara out there in the middle of the Mojave, I already knew her. She was the embodiment of all that the bicycle has meant to me—escape, physical empowerment, and ultimately a rediscovery of my imagination in landscape. Barbara, that bicycle-riding survivor, has always been my companion, a phantom rider on every bike ride I have ever taken and ever will take. She represents the extreme landscape of my inner journeys, the hot and rocky parts to cross on my eventual return home.

On Being at Sea

Sarah died at a time in my life when I had come to terms, more or less, with the basic challenges of my youth. My books were getting published and I'd found a partner who made me laugh everyday. It was a life I felt I had created, willed into existence out of the tangle of childhood. But the idea of will felt wiped out by the fact of death. Sarah's dying didn't precipitate that blizzardy crisis in Hope Valley—that had been a lifetime in coming—but her death did unmoor me, cast me out to sea. Literally.

Pat and I flew to the Dominican Republic, which shares a small island with Haiti, an island that separates the Caribbean Sea from the Atlantic Ocean. At the airport, we threw our duffels into the trunk of a cab and fell into the back seat. Pat told the driver we would like to go to the old port, *puerto viejo*. He revved the engine, pulled out of the tiny airport and said, *"Sí, puerto nuevo,"* thereby beginning a long argument in Spanish between Pat and the cab driver about which port we wanted. I agreed with the cab driver: by all means, let's go to the new port. Why would we want the old one, the one, judging by the cab driver's reaction, that was no longer in use?

I joined in the fray by singing out, *"Challenge of New England! Challenge of New England!"* which was the name of the vessel we hoped to meet. Maybe he had seen the American schooner in one of the ports and would know exactly where to take us. But Pat suggested I let her handle this and pursued her *puerto viejo* line, over and over again, until the driver shrugged and fell silent.

As we sliced through the night on a one-lane road, the hot wet air washing our faces through the open windows, I stared out into the jungle. Now and then we flew by festively lit cabanas, their colors a bright blur in the night. I saw men wearing dark trousers and white undershirts, holding Coca Cola or beer bottles, and wished we could stop for a cold drink. Wished, in fact, that we could stay in the Dominican Republic and explore its beaches, towns, cabanas, and native beers rather than get on the boat in whichever port and sail into the Atlantic.

I like the earth beneath my feet. The idea of bobbing about in a wooden boat in the immensity of the sea frightens me. After all, we know more about the surface of the moon than the murky sea depths. Pat, on the other hand, loves the water and sailing second only to music and her trombone. She'd taught sailing for many years on Cape Cod and in England and always wanted us to take a sailing trip some time. When this one was offered for free, Pat was ecstatic and I acquiesced. I bolstered myself for the trip by trying to think of it as just another kind of adventure. After all, I love high mountains and deep forests. The sea would be a new wilderness challenge. Who was I to say no to the Caribbean? We had been promised island hopping, beach combing, swimming, and whale watching. I prepared myself for long afternoons lying on the deck reading books while the sails slapped lazily overhead and the wind ruffled my tank top. So I gave in to this trip, and that's one of the things I love best about travel, giving in. The loss of control. The feeling of being truly on a ride. Of being at sea.

The stretches between the lit-up cabanas grew longer and longer until there was nothing but black sky and thick vegetation, both threatening to swallow the road. Then, in what appeared to be the middle of the jungle, the cab driver pulled over, turned around to face us in the back seat and said, *"Puerto viejo."* He had tired eyes and baggy cheeks. I could tell that he hoped we understood that this destination was our fault, not his. Peering out the open window of the cab I saw a pile of old railroad ties and, looming in the near distance, what looked like a deserted warehouse.

I asked Pat, "Should we get out?"

For reasons I still don't understand, she was perfectly confident that we were in the right place. It wasn't until I crawled out of the back seat that I saw that there was indeed a port on the far side of the cab. A few boats rocked gently in the doll-sized harbor. One small wooden ramp led from the pile of railroad ties down to the inky black water. Then what?

Pat had her wallet out and was trying to pay the cab driver, who was hesitant to leave, when footsteps and then deep voices, clearly belonging to at least two big men, emerged from the blackness behind the pile of railroad ties. The cab driver yanked my duffel out of my hand and threw it back into the trunk of the cab. *Get in, get in, get in,* his hand motions urged.

Then one gravelly voice said, *"Challenge of New England?"*

"Yes!" we cried with relief.

"It's okay," I told the cab driver in English. "We know them."

Not exactly true, but true enough. Pat tried to assure him in Spanish.

I pointed to the black harbor, smiled, and said, *"Challenge of New England."*

The cab driver looked over the two burly men who were now pulling my duffel back out of the trunk and taking Pat's bag from her hands. He gave his two crazy American women one last glance, scornful this time, as if he'd suddenly pitched his concern for us far out to sea, accepted his big tip, and drove away.

The men introduced themselves as Jack and Jake and told us that we were the last of the boat's hands to arrive. Passengers, they meant, not hands. But I found the mistake charming in a boaty kind of way. They were the real thing, these sailors, with salty New England accents and what might have been called coarse manners in a nineteenth-century novel.

We followed Jack and Jake down the rickety wooden plank to the tiny dock. Up close I could see that a rowboat was tied to the end of it. As instructed, I climbed in and took a seat at the back. Jake or Jack handed me my book-laden duffel to hold in my lap. Soon we were being rowed through the old Dominican harbor to a vessel anchored a couple of hundred yards out, and finally I opened up to the adventure. The old port, indeed. Why had I wanted anything else? Here there were no cruise ships, no tankers, no yachts, nothing but a couple of dozen small vessels, mostly fishing boats, anchored for the night in a port lit only by lanterns swinging off the masts. Merengue music, coming from one of the boats, spiced the warm air. As the *Challenge of New England,* the biggest boat in port, came into view, I dragged a hand through the water and realized how lucky I was. No matter who this Jake and this Jack were, no matter who else we would enjoy or endure on this seventy-five-foot schooner, I was in the Caribbean for two weeks.

A long rope ladder hung from the deck of the *Challenge of New England* into the sea. I slung the handles of my duffle over my shoulder and began climbing aboard.

Sarah had died of lymphoma during my care shift. Her sister Louise and her brother Dan were also there. Sarah loved her family and I'd heard hours of stories about all of them, but especially about Dan. Cavalier and a bit of a drifter, Dan captained boats around the world. Drinking the fine wines of absentee yacht owners for whom he worked, sailing in and out of exotic ports, knowing everything there was to know about the sea, he had always sounded like a character from an old-fashioned folktale. The Dan I met, however, was an emotional, grief-struck man. He'd arrived from out of town literally moments before Sarah died—that touch of both luck and irresponsibility that seemed typical of the man—and I was impressed by his openness and particularly his ease with death. Shortly after Sarah died, as we all waited for the coroner, we drank Scotch and told stories about Sarah. The Sarah that Louise and Dan knew was a big sister, so different in many ways from the one I knew. I was struck by how little you can ever know of a person from your single perspective.

The coroners finally arrived, a man and woman who each wore dark pants, a white shirt, and a black overcoat. Was it necessary for coroners to look so sinister? I forced myself to watch them carry Sarah out on a board wrapped in a blanket and slide her into their truck. After the coroners left, so did I, so that the family could be alone.

The next time I saw Dan was a week later at Sarah's memorial service. We talked about Sarah and about sailing. Pat egged him on, asked endless questions about his boat and the passengers who paid big bucks for the chance to be at sea and hopefully spot whales. She wrote down the dates of his next sails while I silently wondered why she was leading him to believe we might actually join him on one of these trips and how she thought we could afford it.

But then, in the beginning of February, we got a call from Dan. He needed to take the boat from Puerto Plata in the Dominican Republic, where one trip ended, to St. Thomas in the American Virgin Islands, where another trip would begin. Would we be interested in coming along as his guests on this two-week transport?

As we reached the deck of the boat and dropped our duffels, mine hard and heavy with all the books I planned to read while lounging in the sun for two weeks, a couple of people stopped to stare. The *Challenge of New England,* a replica of a nineteenth-century fishing schooner, belonged to a sailing school and sailed out of a port in Rhode Island. The rest of the folks on board for this transport were volunteers from the sailing school. Pat and I understood that they all knew each other, more or less, and that we were newcomers, but by their alarmed looks, it seemed that they hadn't been forewarned that two Californians were joining them.

"Challenge of New England?" one person after another queried, certain that we'd stepped onto the wrong boat, until finally someone went to alert the captain. When he arrived, the others watched with undisguised surprise at his warm reception of us. Pat and I, in our too-brightly-colored clothes, too-shortly-cropped hair, over-boisterous personalities just didn't jibe with New England understatement. And that Dan, cowboy of the high seas, embraced us, not just physically but totally, apparently shocked them. To me, Dan was simply the brother of my friend who'd just died, but to the rest of the boat he was Captain, a title I quickly learned garnered a lot of respect and power. One didn't question the captain, disturb his sleep, interrupt his sentences, nor step in his path. Unfortunately for me, I never got the hang of viewing Dan as anything but Sarah's baby brother.

"Want to pick your bunks?" Dan asked.

I nodded and gave Pat a wary look: for the two weeks prior to the trip I'd been preoccupied with where we'd sleep. Would I be able to stretch out fully? Would it be clean? Would it be private? Would we be sleeping together? This was, after all, our vacation.

"Let's go see what's left," Dan said.

I didn't like that phrase "what's left." Pat had promised me one thing about this trip and that was that I'd get to sleep undisturbed every night. I'd heard enough sailing stories to know that middle of the night duties were not uncommon, but Pat assured me that while we might be called upon to help with dishes or, at worst, clean the heads, we would not be expected to do anything other than sleep at night. I imagined it being like Girl Scout camp, maybe we'd learn to tie knots and be required to memorize the Beaufort scale, that was all.

The fo'c'sle, which I'd been told was the best place to sleep, was already full, so we proceeded down the ladder to the main salon where the rest of the bunks lined two walls on either side of the dining table. The galley took up one end of the main salon and the cook was at work clanging pots and batting steam away from a big vat. A stench of hot, salty stew filled the small woody cavern. The boat was no luxury liner, that much was clear.

The benches on either side of the dining table doubled as dressing benches for the bunks. Dan showed us the two available berths, both bottom bunks and each with its own curtain that could be closed for privacy. Thank god for small favors. I pulled back the curtain to have a look. The bunk was a wooden pallet, or more like a wooden cradle, for the curving inside of the hull formed the back wall. Which I found a little alarming. Was there nothing more than these hull planks separating the sleeper from the sea? I could hear little slapping sounds of the water against the boat, which told me more than I wanted to know. The eighteen inches of vertical clearance explained why the top bunks were all gone and made it evident that I wouldn't be dressing in the bunk, probably not even sleeping on my side. I started to remove the huge duffel someone had thrown in my bunk.

"That's your emergency duffel," Dan said. "Everyone has one. It holds a life preserver, a wet suit, and other survival equipment. It, along with all other personal possessions, must remain in your bunk at all times."

"I see." I patted the rock hard duffle, which took up considerably more than half the bunk. About the size of a big body. So I wouldn't be sleeping alone. I threw in my own duffel and eyed what little remained of the space. Maybe at night I could shove one of the duffels under the dining room table. I turned to check out that space just in time to see Dan squash a cockroach scuttling across the top of the table—a mere two feet from the head of my bunk. It made a hard crunching sound.

"Sorry," he apologized. "We have a bit of an infestation."

An *infestation?*

He flashed his boyish grin, the one that dared any wimps aboard to object, then distracted us by offering beers, welcome on this hot night. My clothes, which I'd been wearing since I left home, were soaked through from the humidity.

As we climbed back up the ladder, cold beers in hand, two or three faces peered from behind bunk curtains. I knew we stood out a little, but were we *that* interesting?

On deck, where the air was hot and wet but at least fresh, we leaned over the railing and looked into the water. I felt relief in being with Dan, as if his blood relation to Sarah brought her back just a little bit. None of us had mentioned her yet, but she was why we were here, why we all were able to bridge time, big geographical spaces, and even bigger cultural spaces to be together now, leaning over this railing looking into a Caribbean harbor. The sky was a soup of stars and as we talked, quietly, a big half moon, as orange as cantaloupe flesh, rose over the island, fat side down and flat side up. I could still hear faint merengue music along with the lapping of the sea against the boat's hull.

Dan told us about a seventy-knot squall the *Challenge of New England* had encountered on Sarah's birthday. The wind had howled through the rigging at such a pitch that he and the crew had had to scream in one another's ears to be heard. When Dan ordered the crew to bring down the headsails, he left the helm with a passenger for a moment, giving strict orders as to the boat's course, so he could go forward to help. When he felt the boat heading down—too far down—he raced back to the helm to head her up, but he was too late. The foresail jibed and the foresail gaff cracked against the shrouds and broke in two.

"What a shame," I said politely, wondering what a gaff was. "Did you get it fixed?"

Dan pointed out the telephone pole–sized beam, one end torn raw, now lashed to the deck.

"That's the gaff?" Surely a part that size was not optional.

Dan agreed that this three-hundred-pound, twenty-four-foot-long log was a critical piece of equipment, but seemed cheerful enough. Another one of those get-back-on-the-horse grins. I'd already learned that one didn't ask the captain too many questions, even if he was the little brother of your good friend, and so I didn't ask again what sailing gaff-less meant for us. Excited by last week's adventure, Dan told us more sea stories about boats "just like this one" that went down in years past and exactly how the disasters had happened.

His stories, and the somewhat disabled boat, made me reconsider my romantic view of the *puerto viejo*. Was our mooring here a financial decision? Was this where second-rate boats anchored? Were we hiding from more stringent inspections that might take place at the *puerto nuevo*?

Ah, but on a night like this it was hard to worry for long. A light breeze rocked the lanterns on the boats in the harbor and the plump orange moon rose higher and higher. In a setting this mellow, a storm was hard to imagine. The merengue music begged me to loosen up, relax, take this trip one day at a time. Okay, I told the moon, the lanterns, the black sea, and the music, count me in.

Later that evening Dan called a meeting on the quarterdeck and he introduced Pat and me as his "special guests." I enjoyed the perplexed expressions of the other people on board as they tried to figure out the alliance between these two wild women and the handsome captain. I was beginning to realize that it would be fun being in the charmed sphere of the captain, how the crew and other passengers deferred to him, and by extension, to us.

Unfortunately, Dan ruined my improving mood by mentioning another hitch. His crew had all gotten sick off the last water they'd obtained in Puerto Plata. He didn't think it was a problem, but if we were fussy we had two hours to row into town to buy bottled water for the two-week voyage.

My throat contracted in panic. I love water. *Fresh* water. I drink a couple of quarts a day, and that's in a cool climate. Even if I could purchase six gallons of water, even if I could carry them up the rope ladder onto the boat, they would take up the last few square feet left in my bunk. Besides, I didn't want to leave the boat now that we'd finally gotten on it.

Luckily, a self-appointed group decided to go ashore for water and took orders. Pat and I asked for three gallons between us, and when they returned, I stowed two of the precious jugs behind my emergency duffle and one behind Pat's. Finally, it was time for bed.

I was barely speaking to Pat by now—so far, the magical aspects of the trip fell short of making up for the cockroaches, broken gaff, and poisoned water—so I climbed into bed without even saying goodnight. I lay in my sweaty bunk, which felt more like a bookshelf, suspended in a kind of wet stupor, and wondered how it was that I had a partner who was happiest at sea level while I was happiest at ten thousand feet.

Periodically, I tried different positions with my bunkmate, the emergency duffel, until I fell asleep.

At 2:45 a.m. someone yanked open my curtain. A large man loomed in the space. Luckily I'm not trained in any self-defense techniques or I might have clobbered him.

Jack said, "You're on my watch. We're on at three."

He had to be kidding.

I managed to say it, "You have to be kidding." During the meeting on the quarterdeck Dan had called out the names of the different

32

watches, but I was still working with the Girl Scout camp model and assumed that the formation of these watches was to give us the feel of being true sailors—the *feel*, not the real thing.

Jack moved on to the next bunk over and was giving Pat the same story.

"Let's go," he said, heading up the ladder to the deck.

Leaning out of my bunk, I glared at Pat. "I'm sleeping."

"You have to get up," she said.

It was the captain thing again, ship protocol. One didn't say, "No, I don't feel like it." I began to realize that this wasn't Girl Scout camp.

"You're kidding," I tried one last time, waiting for the heaving in my stomach, a result of the boat's motion plus being awakened in the middle of the night, to subside.

"It'll be fun. Come on." She nudged me up the ladder.

The moment I hit the deck, I revived. My boxer shorts and tank top—yes, I stumbled up to the deck in my pajamas—were soaked through with sweat but the night air up there was cool and plentiful. The sky was full of stars and the sea looked velvety. We reported to the quarterdeck where the first mate, Mary, explained our duties. One of us was to be stationed at all times at the bow on the lookout for other ships, which of course was not necessary tonight as we hadn't left the harbor. We were to take turns making hourly boat checks, which included checking each of the heads and bilges. The bilges, she explained, were a particularly important point of inspection because there was a leak somewhere in the boat.

"What?" I woke up a little more.

The strict look she fastened on me conveyed another ship lesson: When the first mate was talking, it wasn't a discussion, it was an order. "The bilges are filling too quickly, ergo a leak. Got it?"

I resisted the urge to salute.

As she continued with directives for our four-hour watch, I obsessed about the ergo a leak. Was this commonplace? To be at sea with a leak that filled things called bilges? I looked at Pat who refused to look back at me. Mary assigned posts and charged me with the first engine check.

"Do you need help?" she wanted to know.

Help? Oh, no, I've been a boat mechanic for years. I'll "check" the engine, no problem. "Yes, thank you," I said as servilely as possible.

Mary marched off toward the engine room and I followed. We descended into the belly of the ship, ducking through narrow passageways, until she opened a small door and stepped onto a tiny, cramped wooden platform, barely big enough for the two of us. The engine, an elephant-sized piece of machinery covered with knobs, handles, and dials, looked like a sea monster encrusted with barnacles. Mary yanked a huge pair of padded vinyl ear muffs off a hook and popped them over my ears. I read her lips as she said these were to protect my ears when the engine was on, which it wasn't tonight of course because we were still on the anchor. She rapped her knuckles on the steel body and I yanked off the ear muffs in time to hear her say, "When this baby's on, she's hot enough to sear your flesh." I could just see it: the boat hits a wave, I'm tossed onto the engine where my skin grafts to the steel. Talking fast, she pointed to the dials and gauges and switches, explaining their importance and how to read them. I was to record all my findings in the notebook attached to the clipboard that hung on a nail next to the ear muffs. I pretended to understand every word of her instructions so I could get out of that claustrophobic pit as fast as possible. I did try to concentrate on which switches to flip when and which set of numbers—all the instruments seemed to have several—I was supposed to record.

"Got it?" Mary asked.

"Sure," I said.

"Okay, then go ahead and do the first engine check."

"But we're not moving. What's to check?"

Another withering look. I did the engine check.

I spent the rest of the watch marching up and down the deck "keeping an eye out." For what, I couldn't imagine. I was dying to go back to sleep. How was it that I suddenly found myself in this minuscule harbor off a tiny island in the middle of the Atlantic Ocean performing paramilitary-type duties? In my underwear.

It was Sarah's fault. When someone dies, particularly someone young, survivors always vow to live now, waste nothing, not hold back. It's like a spell that envelops you for a while. Come sail in the Caribbean? You bet. Don't ask questions, just buy the plane ticket. Live now.

As I paced the deck, trying to look like I was carrying out orders, I allowed that—as sleepy as I was, as unpleasant as the thought of returning to that engine room was—this particular moment, my current now, wasn't all that bad. How could I complain about watching a Caribbean dawn from the deck of a sailboat in an island harbor?

At seven my watch was finally sent below for sleep. I crawled into my damp, sandy bookshelf and passed out. By the time I emerged several hours later, the dawn had bloomed into a gorgeous day. No sooner had I rubbed my eyes and taken a few experimental steps on deck, than Captain Dan ordered the anchor raised and the sails hoisted. The crew hustled to get us underway. The sails snapped into place, sunny and bright, and we clipped along at a good pace out of the harbor and into the open sea. The cook climbed the ladder to announce that he'd made a fresh pot of coffee, my dearest wish come true, and I sipped a big mug of it as the Dominican Republic shrank and finally disappeared off the stern. I went below to get my notebook and pen, and then found a place on deck where I could nestle out of the wind to write. Now and then I heard Pat's voice, enthusiastically volunteering for a variety of activities, happy and carefree. She hurried by on the heels of the first mate to help pull some line, and I loved her in spite of my bondage on this adventure of hers.

I applied a layer of sun screen and tried to write up the details of my first twelve hours on board. The unwieldy sky and sea made it hard to concentrate. I felt as if my mind expanded to fill the space, spreading my brain cells out too thin for solid ideas to form. I wrote a few words—cockroach, engine check, miraculous dawn—hopefully to prompt full sentences later, then gave in to the daze.

I had reached a catlike state of meditative napping when I heard the first mate's voice calling from the other end of the boat, "All hands on deck! All hands on deck!"

I was a guest, not a hand, so I stayed nestled where I was.

"Lucy!" Mary the first mate appeared, pointing at my nose. "All hands on deck."

Wait a minute. Wait just one minute. I was invited, not hired, for this voyage. . . . I could ignore the obvious no longer. Apparently, I was a hand.

I barely had time to duck below and stow my notebook in my bunk. As I ascended the ladder to the deck, someone tossed a sponge at my chest. A bucket of water splashed at my feet. "Deck-swabbing," Jake informed. Over the course of the next couple of hours, we scrubbed every inch of wood on the deck. A couple lucky sailors had the fun job of rinsing everything in sight with the fire hoses and water pumped from the sea, but the rest of us worked like dogs.

The wind picked up and my stomach began tossing with the waves. Wind, of course, was something to celebrate on a sailboat, but by the time we finished scrubbing the deck I felt like a sick cartoon character with X's for eyes as I lurched about. The cook had made a lunch of chili and homemade oatmeal cookies which I went below to eat, hoping it would settle my stomach. Luckily the food was good and I tried to focus on the nice flavors on my palate while keeping a lookout for cockroaches and gripping the table to keep from being thrown off the bench. I washed down the meal with "punch," the sickly sweet drink of varying colors that would accompany every meal and which I felt compelled to drink because it preserved my jugs of water. The close, hot air of the main salon made me feel sicker, so immediately following lunch I headed up the ladder again.

No longer expecting leisure, I stood on deck and waited for the next torturous chore to be announced. The boat rocked and heaved, a motion that back home I'd fantasized as being nurturing, soothing, hypnotic, but which instead was one of the most unsettling feelings imaginable. We'd been warned to never vomit in the heads but to weave our arms in the ratlines, to avoid going overboard, while delivering the contents of our stomachs to Neptune. Now as I watched my fellow shipmates hurling their lunches into the sea, an extreme nausea overpowered me. I wasn't about to throw up in front of all these strangers, so I charged down the ladder to the main salon and thankfully found the head unoccupied. The nice thing about throwing up in the head, besides the satisfaction of being insubordinate, was that the place was so disgusting you never had to wait for the impulse to realize itself—response was immediate. I pumped the head empty and managed to get into my bunk. I hunkered there hoping no one summoned me for more labor.

The nausea I felt was akin to the kind that accompanies a migraine. The boat was tossing and the air was fetid, a kind of chili-flavored salt stench. I felt both greasy and sticky, and my eyes were crusty. At some point Pat came to get something from her bunk and I waved an arm out my curtain. She poked her head in, grinning, apparently having the time of her life. How could her perfect day be my nightmare?

"I've never sailed in such an ideal breeze," she enthused.

That did it. Her euphoria was like pouring gas on the fire of my misery. I said, "Land. Now."

She tried to pet my hair but I swatted her hand away.

"You tell Dan. Go tell him now. First island. I'm off this boat."

She nodded, and I saw her thinking.

"I mean it. I can't go on."

"Okay, honey."

"Don't okay honey me. I'm not joking."

"Okay, okay."

"You'll talk to him? You don't have to get off with me. I'm sure they have an airport of some sort on all of these—"

Here it came again. I bowled her aside and charged to the head. In use. Up the ladder, gagging, spitting, stumbling across the deck, heaving over the railing. So much for not throwing up in front of strangers.

"Your arms in the rigging!" First mate Mary, whose eyes seemed to cover every inch of this seventy-five-foot boat, corrected my vomiting technique. She yanked one of my arms off the railing and jabbed it in the rigging for me. That time I heaved correctly.

Having come to terms with the fact that I was a hand and not a passenger, I made it through the next couple of days. No one put me ashore as requested and I didn't ask again. I even had some good times. Like the day Captain Dan ordered all hands in the sea and we jumped overboard for a swim—oh, to rinse the salt crust and galley grease from my skin—in the middle of the Atlantic, no land in sight, where the bottom was two and a half miles below. Mary the first mate climbed the mast and stood lookout while we swam. "Lookout for what?" I asked. "Sharks," Dan grinned. I wrote "sharks" in my notebook that night.

There were more highlights. We spotted whales, Pat played her trombone on the bow at sunset, and I climbed the rigging. The sails were up, we were clipping along at four or five knots, and Captain Dan went first. I put one sneaker on the rope crosspiece, pulled with my arms and kept climbing. The boat was heeling over at a nice angle and when I looked down, I looked into a thirty yard drop to the deep blue. On deck, the crew and other hands craned their necks watching. Finally, three-quarters of the way to the top, I froze. Up here, the ratlines were four inches apart, barely room to stuff my sneaker toe between them, and nothing to lean my body against. Dan, now standing on the platform at the top, shouted down for me to hook my harness to the rigging. I shouted back that I wasn't letting go of the ratlines to hook anything. He looked surprised—at my talking back—but just laughed. This time.

On the fifth day, the main starboard spreader broke. This piece of equipment spreads the shrouds and supports the mast, even less optional functions than that once performed by the broken gaff. Dan and a couple of crew members spent five hours rigging a make-shift replacement. The skies darkened over the course of that after-noon, a rat was reported to be on the loose in the fo'c'sle, and the bilges were filling more quickly than ever.

And my watch had another graveyard shift coming on that night.

By now I was slaphappy from the total loss of control over my destiny, that drunken feeling of being able to do absolutely nothing about the situation in which you find yourself. I was in the hands of Dan our cavalier captain and in the arms of the *Challenge of New England,* our disabled nineteenth-century replica. I'd come to be grate-ful for Mary, the rulebook first mate, but didn't really think her sharp adherence to ship protocol could make up for the leaks and broken parts. Not to mention poisoned water, cockroaches, and rats.

So Pat and I approached our upcoming 11 p.m. to 3 a.m. watch with a little unrestrained joviality. "Party watch," we told the other hands at supper, "coming on at eleven o'clock. All comers welcome."

No one laughed.

By the time supper was finished, the breeze had quickened to a more challenging blow. The sky was a palette of grays, billowing fig-ures sculpted from clouds. I'd never seen a sky so actively in motion. Pat and I hit the sack right after supper to be as rested as possible for our party watch. By the time we were awakened at ten-forty-five, the boat was really heaving. The waves pounded the hull next to my head and all the timbers were creaking like some Halloween opera. When we arrived on deck, I was surprised to find that only a light rain spit down on us and the wind causing all that racket below wasn't as forceful as it sounded. The sea, however, roiled like a bad mood.

"Would you be comfortable at the helm?" Mary the first mate asked me.

"Uh," I said. "Well, I'm not sure, uh . . ."

"It's not a multiple-choice question," she snapped. "Yes or no."

I remembered Dan's story about the passenger at the helm when the gaff snapped. "No."

She assigned the helm to Jack and sent me to the front of the boat for lookout. "Stay off the bow," she warned me. "Wrap your arms in the shrouds and watch from there. We don't need anyone overboard in this weather."

The boat rose on the crests then plunged into the troughs, rocking from side to side like an enormous cradle. Each time the boat's bow crashed back down, a spray of sea water rained onto the deck. I stood with my arms woven into the rigging, hurling position, although I no longer felt sick, and stared out into the black storm. Did Jack know how to steer a boat? Shouldn't someone wake the captain when the sea gets this rough?

Occasionally Jake stumbled forward to check on me. Once he pointed into the mess of sea, rain, and cloud. "Puerto Rico," he shouted to be heard. "We're about fifteen miles off its lee shore." What happened, I wondered, to the coconut beaches? I distinctly remember hearing about a wonderful market in Puerto Rico where we were going to shop. When was the island-hopping portion of the trip going to begin?

By one in the morning we were ripping along at about nine knots and plowing through eight-foot waves. I pressed my chest against the shrouds and rode the ship like some giant beast. One squall after another blew through, and I held on, staring as deeply into the night as I could, looking for any red, green, or white lights, signals from other ships at sea. I kept hearing voices and turned time and again, expecting Pat or Jack or Jake, but no one was ever there. I heard a dog barking, too, as distinct and clear as if it were a few yards away on deck. I shook my head and tried to focus on my task. But the harder I tried to concentrate, the more active my imagination became. Or was it imagination? Songs, animal sounds, whole conversations wafted from the rigging and sails and deck planks. It was as if the ship was inhabited by a multitude of poor souls, permanently lost at sea like some kind of purgatory, who were taking refuge on the *Challenge of New England* for the duration of the storm. Bad choice of vessel, I wanted to tell them. You're likely to reexperience a trauma similar to the one that trapped you out here in the first place. Nevertheless, I was happy for, rather than spooked by, the company. After a bit, I tried to sing and bark along.

Then the waves began cresting the side of the boat and splashing onto the deck. We weren't playing at sailing now, these were real squalls, each one blowing in fiercer than the one before. I might have been frightened except that as each wave receded and the water spilled back into the sea, the entire deck glittered with blue-green sparkles. The water was teeming with bioluminescent critters. When the next wave doused the deck, I scooped up a handful of sea water and the organisms pulsed in my hands like bitsy stars.

"Do you see that light?" This time the voice was real. Mary the first mate was at my side.

"They're beautiful," I said, dreamy and mesmerized in spite of a bigger-than-ever wave crashing onto the deck, knocking me away from the shrouds because I'd taken my arms out to gather up the sea water in my hands.

Her voice felt like a slap. "Not the deck," she shouted. "That light. Out there." She pointed at the sea-sky, for on this stormy night it was all one, off the port side of the bow.

"What light?"

"That's a ship. It's your job to spot anything coming."

I peered into the black wetness of rain and waves and saw nothing. I couldn't see a ship, a light, anything out there. I really couldn't. Besides, I wanted to know but didn't dare ask: didn't they have instruments that detected oncoming vessels? I mean, I knew we were simulating sailing in another century, but didn't they hide a computer in one of those antique cabinets? Just for safety's sake? Were they really depending on me to avoid a collision in this squall? Surely the *Challenge of New England* was equipped with modern instrumentation.

Exasperated, Mary strode back to the quarterdeck. I was impressed with how the true sailors on board could walk, without lurching or staggering, on a boat this wildly in motion. A moment later, Jake appeared to replace me. I reported back to the quarterdeck where I found Jack and Pat sitting on the deckhouse quietly cracking jokes while a few yards away Mary stood at the helm. "Party watch," I said and the jokes got louder. The rain pummeled our slickers and the waves swept onto the boat, but still we laughed, then began singing, until Mary told us to shut up. The captain was trying to sleep.

So I clutched anything stable I could find on the boat and rode out the watch, forced back to more serious thoughts, like why I was here in the first place and whether this storm would deliver me to the same place Sarah now resided. I thought of the storm the day of Sarah's birthday, the day the gaff broke, and I thought of Sarah's rage at the end of her illness and how like her it would be to express it— who knew what powers you got at death?—in the form of a storm.

At three o'clock, the party watch was released and we went down to bed. The storm sounded much scarier below, the timbers groaning and squealing, the salt and pepper shakers stored in a little shoot on the tabletop sliding back and forth, back and forth. It sounded as if the boat was breaking apart, and I had every reason to believe by now that that was possible. Upon crawling in my bunk, I discovered that half of my duffel was soaked, the half that lay up against the inside of the hull. I quickly checked my two jugs of water. Both were capped tightly, sat upright, and were bone dry. The water wetting my duffel had come from the sea, through these hull planks and into my bunk. I thought of the ever-filling bilges, and then decided that if we were going down, I wanted it to happen in my sleep. I didn't run my hands along the planks to feel for leaking water. Instead, I nestled up to my two duffels and willed myself to lose consciousness. As the waves battered the planks at my ear and pitched me back and forth in the bunk, my last thought was to wonder how long until the planks busted open and let in the sea.

When I returned to the deck around noon the next day, I found gray skies and a strong breeze but easy seas. Captain Dan and I had a cup of coffee together, and I learned that the storm had worsened after my watch. He'd finally arisen and taken the helm. I realized, listening to his immense relief, that I should have been even more scared than I had been. Then he announced that we were close to Charlotte Amalie, the harbor in St. Thomas.

"You mean a few days?"

"A few hours."

I was floored. How could that be? We had signed up for a two-week sail. This was the beginning of day six. What had happened to coconut islands? Beer under cabanas? After a brief moment of feeling cheated, I switched to overjoyed. Oh, get me off this barely-floating pile of planks!

Information had been hard to come by on the *Challenge of New England,* but Dan now allowed that we'd sailed straight through, as fast as possible, because of the condition of the boat. He planned to pull her out on one of the Virgin Islands and look for the leak, or leaks. We'd made incredible time during the storm and here we were, nearly at our destination. Dan was still in a hurry, though, because a big swell from a gale in the north Atlantic was quickly heading our way. He wanted to get in protected waters before the twenty-knot easterlies, headwinds for us, stopped us dead.

"It's no problem," he said. "You and Pat can stay onboard after we pull out. A little daytime help sanding and painting the hull, and you can have your bunks and meals for free."

I almost laughed in his face. Even if we were about to be stranded for eight days in one of the most expensive places in the world, I'd be damned if I was going to sand and paint a boat hull, in tropical heat, on my vacation. Or sleep in that stinky main salon another eight nights. "I don't think so," I told Dan.

"What do you mean? You're deserting us?" His tone implied we owed him. He also looked a little trapped, both angry and as if he might cry.

"Not deserting," I said firmly. "Disembarking. In St. Thomas."

The next day we motored into Charlotte Amalie and dropped anchor. While Dan took the dingy into customs with all our passports, I leaned on the boat's railing and gazed at the town. My feet throbbed with desire for land.

But it was late by the time all the arrangements had been made with customs and we would have to wait until morning to disembark. That evening at supper, which we all ate in the main salon because it was raining again, Dan called a meeting. He wanted to organize a watch schedule for the time we were in the harbor. Since most of the folks on board expressed an interest in going ashore to drink, I volunteered to watch the boat until midnight.

Dan said, "Harbor watches are for twelve hours. That'll be from seven tonight until seven in the morning."

I said, "No. I offered the evening. Someone else will have to do the late shift."

A strange smile, part amused and part enraged, settled on Dan's face and his body stiffened. It seemed like a small matter to me, my pointing out what I'd offered—kindly, I thought, accommodating the desires of the others—but the tense reaction of the entire crew and the volunteers let me know that I'd stumbled into dangerous territory. You just didn't say no to the captain, it wasn't done, no matter that he's your friend's little brother, no matter that you're getting off the ship in twelve hours. Maybe, too, he was angry that his sister had died and we, what he had left of her, were not only leaving but defying him.

His voiced strained, sounding like a sea lion's bark, "Lucy and Pat on watch from seven until seven. And check the bilges every hour. You'll probably have to pump them."

"Oh, come *on*," I said. I understood the importance of a strict line of command while at sea, the necessity of a stringent set of procedures, how these save lives, but we were anchored in the harbor at St. Thomas. We were talking about who got to go into town to drink and for how long. There were twenty-five people aboard. Why were we the only ones to work the entire night?

"Galley duty goes to Lucy and Pat, too," Dan said. "Meeting's over."

"No." My voice boomed out once again. Dan turned to talk with one of the deck hands and ignored me.

Now I was the one who was enraged. How had my offering a favor been turned into receiving a punishment?

"I'll do galley duty," Jack said quietly, and a couple of others piped up that they'd help, but Dan, overhearing, interrupted his private conversation to say, "No, Lucy and Pat will do it."

I was so angry that my eyes filled with tears. I could accept that we'd just worked our butts off for five days. I could even accept that for months we'd be paying off credit card bills for a Virgin Islands holiday we hadn't chosen. After all, I had counted on adventure and that meant risk and consequences. But I hadn't counted on Dan being so mean-spirited, and that hurt.

Soon after Pat and I finished the dishes, which several of the guys did help us with, the crew and volunteers descended the rope ladder to the dingy, which they would row to shore for their drinking spree. By now it was pouring rain and I looked forward to going below and reading in my bunk after they were gone. Dan was the last to climb over the boat railing, and as I stood in the rain watching him go he delivered one last order. "Stay on deck tonight. In a harbor like this you have to keep alert."

Twelve hours of pacing the deck in this rain? I didn't think so. I went right to bed and slept through the night.

Not twenty-four hours later, Pat and I sat in our bathing suits on a white sand beach, sipping homemade rum punch from a water bottle. We'd found a campground on St. John where we could rent a tent and cookware, buy supplies from a little store, and bask on a beach that was surrounded by night-blooming honeysuckle and other luscious jungle vegetation. Because the island is a national park, there were no high-rise hotels or condominiums. Not only was it inexpensive, it was the most beautiful tropical setting I could imagine. How quickly one's fortunes flip-flop while traveling.

With solid land beneath me, I was already able to laugh about the *Challenge of New England,* even relish the memories. Now the rat and cockroaches were hilarious; I wouldn't have wanted to do the trip with a foresail gaff or watertight hull. I was delighted—in hindsight—that Pat had taken me on this adventure and thanked her for doing so much of my work, including checking the bilges hourly while I slept soundly in my bunk the rainy night before.

I pushed my heels through the sand and looked out on the Caribbean, spread before me where it was supposed to be, on the outer edge of my personal geography rather than directly below it. As Pat mixed another round of rum punch, I thought about being at sea. How less and less like a captain I felt in my own life. How hard it must be to *be* a captain because people would assume you are in control. How death is the ultimate loss of control. I guess the safety of being on land, the relief in having Pat to myself again, and the effects of the rum punch all went to my head because I felt sorry I had left Dan, my only connection to Sarah, so angrily.

So, a few days later, Pat and I took a ferry to a nearby island, and as our boat pulled into the small harbor, we spotted the dry-docked *Challenge of New England.* Mary the first mate, who was standing on scaffolding, scraping paint off the boat's hull, assumed we'd failed to make it on our own. She made it immediately clear that if we wanted meals, we'd have to work. Before she could give us our assignments, I assured her that we'd come only for a short visit. I wondered if we would be welcome for even that, but a moment later, Captain Dan himself came trotting around from the other side of the boat, grinning his devilish smile, saying that he had heard of our arrival. Despite the oceans of difference between us, Pat and I grinned back, as happy to see him as he seemed to be to see us.

Above Treeline

Ilifted my backpack out of the trunk and propped it against a
tree, pleased that I'd made the trailhead so early in the day.
The sky was an icy autumn blue and a breeze made the golden
aspen leaves talk. Late October, snow would soon fall, could even
fall this week. This would be the last trip of the year during which I'd
feel soil beneath my boots. And the first of the year in which I'd
finally be alone. Most years I make at least two solo trips, one in the
winter and one in the summer, but this year all attempts at solitude
had been thwarted and now my need for it was intense.

As I taped my feet, a Jeep Cherokee towing a horse trailer pulled
into the parking area. I sped up my foot-doctoring. Three men,
sparking with enthusiasm, jumped out of the Cherokee. I've seen
these kinds of guys in the wilderness a lot, making their yearly trip
with the boys, away from wives and children. Two of them looked
like professional family men. The soft blond one had more than the
usual middle-age chubbiness. A lawyer, I guessed. The tall stern one
with square plastic glasses was surely an accountant. I noted the gold
bands on their ring fingers, the expensive wool shirts. The third

man, a guy with a long mustache and shag haircut, looked different. I decided he was a musician, an old college chum of the lawyer and accountant. Behind his back they'd discuss his unwillingness, or perhaps inability, to settle down, how he still lived as if he were twenty. I imagined the lawyer and accountant resenting his independence, their wives liking the handsome, loose musician a little too much. And yet out here in the wilderness he became their center. The family men orbited around his louder, wilder energy. He was the instigator of a good time, the perfect excuse.

"Russell," the lawyer clapped his back, "you're not bringing that whole bottle of brandy, are you?"

Russell grinned. Then he noticed me across the parking lot. "Howdy." His eyes raked across my car, backpack, body. "By yourself?"

Obviously.

Russell kept grinning and glancing at me as he unloaded the fishing poles, then the first gun. I was surprised. These guys didn't look like hunters. The Cherokee and other high-end gear made it clear they didn't need the meat. Hunting for sport appalled me.

But I eat meat, I reminded myself. Doesn't that make me a hunter who lets others do the dirty work?

I have hunted, once. About twenty years ago, on a trip in Alaska's Wrangell Mountains, my hiking partner and I ran out of food. People hunt in Alaska. They think you're out of your mind if you go into the backcountry without a gun. We didn't have a gun, but Wendy and I spent a lot of time on that trip talking about guns and killing. We heartily agreed that hunting was evil and that we could never kill.

Then we got hungry.

After three days of nothing but small portions of oatmeal, the concept of good and evil seemed ridiculously superfluous. Our best bet were ptarmigans, big birds reputed to taste like chicken. They were plentiful in the Wrangell Mountains and, better yet, far too stupid to realize someone was trying to kill them. I'd read that they were easy prey: simply hit them in the head with a rock. The drawback was that these big birds, who sat up on tree branches often no more than ten feet above ground, had tiny heads. Wendy and I, salivating for roast bird, found stones and fired them at the pinheads. I felt no remorse as I tried to kill. Even a little bit of hunger can alter a person in dramatic ways. As it turned out, I never hit my target, though we did get to taste ptarmigan. We soon ran into a trail crew who fed us a breakfast of hot coffee, powdered scrambled eggs, toast, and fire-roasted ptarmigan. It was delicious.

Who was I to judge these guys about to hunt in the Trinity Alps?

I hefted my pack and set out on the Canyon Creek Trail, ignoring Russell's final salutation, figuring I would make tracks to put distance between the guys and me. I felt glad to be hiking. And alone at last.

The air hinted at snow, a feeling of icy warning. With every few hundred feet I gained in elevation, the deciduous leaves changed color. The evergreen boughs sagged, heavy with the year's bumper crop of toasty-brown cones. The undergrowth on either side of the trail rustled with constant noise, the sounds of animals hurrying to pull together the last of their winter stores.

I walked fast and let my mind roar through the complications of the summer. No wonder those men's guns made me uneasy. I had felt hunted earlier in the season during the whole trip in Montana's Beartooth Mountains. My hiking partner, Katie, and I had set out from the Bay Area expecting two weeks of lakes and wildlife and long views. I was apprehensive about going in the crowded month of August, rather than our usual September, but hoped to get off the trail quickly and leave all signs of civilization far behind.

We stopped in Salt Lake to pick up Katie's New Yorker sister, Peggy, at the airport. That night our gear—the tent, stove, boots, backpacks, clothes, hundreds of dollars of food, and much, much more—was ripped off from my car.

I live in the city. I've been mugged, my home has been broken into several times, and cars are picked off my street regularly. These are violations. But my *backpacking* gear. I felt as if the thief had ripped off my soul. I felt hunted.

At least, as I was told by lots of well-meaning folks, gear can be replaced. Well, sort of. I'd collected my backcountry gear over decades. True, some of my stuff should have been replaced, like the threadbare wool pants or the stove that worked only when I said *abracadabra* and tapped on the wind screen three times. But some things, like my rag wool hat that'd been in thirty of the fifty states or the perfect cook pot that no one sells anywhere, couldn't be replaced. My first reaction, which lasted for several days, was that I'd give up backpacking. I wanted to go home. But Katie and Peggy were intent on continuing with the trip, which meant a several-thousand-dollar shopping spree at Salt Lake's REI.

Those hours in REI were a nightmare. I hated all that new-fangled gear we bought and spending that kind of money terrified me (though, in the end, my insurance did pay for it). Already, I knew this wouldn't be a real wilderness trip no matter how deeply we penetrated the Beartooth. My relationship to wilderness has built slowly over several decades. It's not an idea but a lifestyle. I like the gear to be as transparent as possible, serving my backcountry travel but not dominating it. The brand-spanking-new tent, sleeping bag, fleece pants, and polypro underwear made me feel ridiculous, like a made-for-TV explorer.

Once in the wilderness, I relaxed. Though we were hiking during the busiest month of the year, in a popular area, we found solitude by heading off the trail and camping at a gorgeous and secluded high alpine lake. We planned to stay there several nights, exploring the surrounding peaks and high plateaus. On the first afternoon, Katie and Peggy went off fishing, leaving me alone. After hiking and climbing and reading all afternoon, I returned to camp at dusk. On the hillside, not far from our cook area, was a shaggy, white mountain goat. I sat on a small rock outcropping and watched it munch its way down the hillside—toward me.

I was amazed the goat didn't run away. They're the shyest mountain animals. You're lucky to see them at a distance. I credited myself for creating this special opportunity. I've always had an affinity with animals. I'm the one who everyone's cat chooses to sit on. Now the mountain goat was just ten yards away. This was the magical moment that would unlock all the distress of the trip. The goat had lovely curving horns and neat little hooves. Its coat was long and elegantly snowy.

Then the goat came yet closer and I became a little uncomfortable. For one, I couldn't help but notice its obscenely large balls. Billy goat balls. The look in its eyes was, well, not exactly hostile, but more like crazed or determined. This was a billy goat gone off in the head. No mountain goats come this close to people.

When my companions returned to our private lake basin carrying a string of rainbow trout, the goat finally scurried back up the hillside. They didn't see him and I didn't tell them about him. I wanted this experience, even if it was a bit deranged, for myself.

That night I slept out alone. There was no moon, just a dark night and a canopy of stars. As I was falling asleep, I heard a grunting sound. I got up on one elbow and saw, not five yards away, a big white phantom. The billy goat with his gargantuan balls. He looked ghostly in the starlight. What was he doing here now? Somehow this whole scene—the boldly sexualized goat haunting me—was reminiscent of the Eastern European folktales I loved as a child. Strange things happened between people and mythical animals. I wanted the goat to leave now but nothing frightened him, not sudden movements nor loud noises. He finally wandered away and I drifted off to sleep for a few minutes. But when I next awoke he was standing by my sleeping bag, gazing down at me.

In the morning I told my hiking partners about the goat and they told me that while fishing they'd met someone who told them about this particular goat. Apparently he was well known. I've heard of camp bears, even camp elk. But camp mountain goats? Even this most elusive, proud species had stooped to become a garbage scavenger. So much for magical moments.

Later that morning, fishermen swarmed over the hill into our private lake basin. They were with an outfit that brought folks in on horses and gave them maps to the best fishing lakes in the Beartooth. Our lake was one.

I gave in and accepted that this trip would have an unexpected cultural component. I even enjoyed chatting with half a dozen of these fishermen. But it wasn't a backcountry experience.

Hightailing it up the Canyon Creek Trail in the Trinity Alps, I realized for the first time that the Beartooth trip might actually make some great stories someday. Someday. At the moment, I wanted only to send those memories on their way into the precise autumn air, send them sailing up into the mountaintops, above treeline, free.

I wanted to make my five days in the Trinity Alps last. So although it was early in the day and I easily could have made it to Upper Canyon Creek Lake, I decided to camp when I found an enchanted meadow with a stream running through it, next to old-growth forest. I wasn't far off-trail, a hundred yards, but it wouldn't matter at this time of year. Who else was here?

My anticipation of a serene afternoon evaporated as quickly as my sweat. I tried to make my camp cozy by setting out the stove and ground cloth, but a column of fear rose inside me. I didn't get it. This easy trip was supposed to be a comfort. After all, I had snow-camped alone, bushwhacked alone, traveled alone in remote parts of the world. This was a warm little trip with a well-marked trail. Fear didn't make sense. Yet I was overwhelmed by it.

I wandered, but the golden late afternoon sunlight on the meadow didn't dislodge the tightness in my chest. I walked in every direction: across the creek into the brush until it was too thick to go on, then along the creek until I encountered a log jam which, another time, I might have delighted in scrambling over. I tried to meditate to the creek's music, then leaned up against an old cedar's thick life, my cheek scraping along its feathery bark. Nothing helped. I could think only about how I had hours ahead of me, alone with this new alienation.

What had happened? Where was the serenity? Why didn't the trees and creek sing away my angst, as they had for so many years? It was as if my very imagination were failing me. Why could I not find a moment of grace here?

By dusk I was sitting on a big boulder in the middle of the meadow, crying. Their voices alerted me. "It's on the other side of the meadow," one called out. I recognized Russell's voice. "Oh, hi!" he shouted, seeing me on the boulder.

I forced a bright smile, feeling like an injured caribou hiding from a wolf. I had to look healthy and capable, and whatever I did, not show fear. Inside, though, I seethed. The three hunters headed across *my* meadow to a campsite that, I gathered from their conversation, they used every year. The Trinity Alps covered thousands of acres and they had to choose a campsite a couple hundred yards from mine? As they hiked past my meadow boulder, I opened my mouth to suggest they move on, but didn't speak. I knew they wouldn't do it; they sagged under their heavy packs. Russell grinned at me. As the horse walked by, it lifted its tail and dropped a large pile next to my boulder.

Listening to the fellows settle into their camp, I waited for darkness, and then crawled into my sleeping bag. Part of my problem, I knew, was exhaustion from several months of intense work. Day one on trips was often difficult. I had four more. Things change, especially my moods.

In the morning I realized that the men wouldn't be going to my destination, Upper Canyon Creek Lake, because it was just above treeline and horses weren't allowed above treeline. I packed up my gear and headed out rather late, thankful for the twelve hours of sleep. The fellows were long gone.

As I climbed the final pitch to Upper Canyon Creek Lake, I began getting excited thinking about where to make camp. The map showed a bar of land between Upper and Lower Canyon Creek Lakes. I hoped to find a spot on that bar where I'd have a long view down the valley. For three days, I'd sit and stare, explore and read.

I crested the hill and got my first look at Upper Canyon Creek Lake. A huge granite wall bordered the far side of the lake. The water looked cold despite the sunshine. I hiked out across the bar of land separating the two lakes and, to my amazement, found the three hunters setting up camp. "Great view," Russell said.

Disappointment strangled my voice as I asked, "Where's your horse?"

Russell pointed down to Lower Canyon Creek Lake. "Tethered down there. We wanted a view." He shook his long hair and ran his hands through it. I noticed his slim hips. Rock musician, I decided. The other two busied themselves with their rifles.

Russell saw me looking at the guns, so I asked, "Deer?"

"Yeah. So far we've gotten one every year." He looked down the valley where the light muted the greens and blues. "I backpack too, but there's nothing like tracking big game. It puts you in relationship with the land like nothing else." He looked me in the eye, challenging. He was more like me than like other hunters, he wanted to tell me. He also wanted me to know that I didn't understand. He was right. I didn't. I've heard the argument before, how hunting provides a deeper, more rigorous wilderness experience, one that makes aimless wandering, the kind I do, look marrowless.

"Have a good trip," I said, as if I didn't know I'd see them again, and then hiked back and forth across the bar of land until I was sure they had the only level campsite. It was getting late. Because of the enormous granite wall on the other side, my only choice was to camp on the small beach on the far end of the lake, below and in full view of the guys. I should have hiked back down to Lower Canyon Creek Lake, but I felt a combination of stubbornness—I wanted to camp at *this* lake—and defeat. What did it matter where I camped? Solitude was possible only in the heart of winter or north of the Arctic Circle.

I had just finished setting up my tent on the spit of beach, as far from the lake as possible, and put on my soup when they came tromping around the lake. They pretended to be taking an evening walk, but I knew they were coming to welcome me to the neighborhood. As they fingered my tent, asked questions about its construction, and commented on the size of my pack, I felt a prickling up my neck. They came in too close, touched too much. I became intensely aware that we were in the wilderness. Playing at being primitive. Hunters. Maybe even animals.

I smelled the brandy, a lot of it, on Russell's breath when he said, "We're building a campfire when we get back to camp. Why don't you join us?" The lawyer and accountant looked out at the lake, maybe embarrassed at their lack of social grace, maybe grateful to Russell for being their spokesperson, maybe wishing he'd shut up.

"Maybe." I was afraid to say no outright.

After they left, my own thoughts struck me as ridiculous. These guys were just friendly chumps out on a camping trip. *They* weren't resentful about sharing the lake with *me.* Their neighborliness made me feel like a cranky old mountain dweller, the kind who made her own liquor and chased people off the land with a shotgun.

Still, all night long I felt like their phantom campfire guest. Their raucous conversation carried across the lake, and though I tried not to listen, I heard "she" and "that girl" several times. Once I clearly heard one, I suspected the righteous, stern accountant, say, "She's out here for some peace and solitude, after all. We should keep it down." After that, they were quiet.

See, I told myself, these guys are even considerate. And yet I didn't sleep in my tent. I set it up as a decoy, then climbed into the boulders above my camp and found a tiny shelf where I spent the night.

Early the next morning, I packed a stuff sack with daytrip supplies and began climbing the ridge above my campsite. I hoped to get a view down into the Stuart Fork, which I'd hiked up a few years before. I'd spent a magical couple of days at Sapphire and Emerald Lakes and wanted to glimpse them today. I never did see them, but it hardly mattered for all the other spectacular views. Yet, for all the climbing and breathing and sweating I did, that heaviness, that plug of unspecified fear, didn't loosen. After tumbling back into camp in the afternoon, I stood looking at the hard, flat surface of the lake and where it stopped at the hard, flat surface of the granite wall on its far side, trying to decide whether to have a snack, take a nap, or read a book.

The gunshot tore open the sky and slammed against the mountainsides.

I moved fast, stuffing my tent, stove, and food bag into the backpack. I knew by the angle at which the light sliced through the cold air that it was too late in the day to move camp, but I was way outside rational. I felt as if I had to outrun the next bullet.

I didn't see the hunters as I skidded down the trail into the valley. They could have been anywhere among the trees, stalking their big game. Or maybe they'd hit an animal with that bullet, and while one man (Russell? the accountant?) butchered, another went to get the horse. The undergrowth was silent now, as if every creature in the area, except for me, was standing perfectly still, awaiting safety.

A couple of miles below Lower Canyon Creek Lake, I saw a faint trail heading up another canyon. I remembered seeing Boulder Lake on the map, settled in a stark basin far above treeline. As I clawed my way up the trail toward Boulder Lake, I thought I could still hear the echo of that explosion ricocheting among the ridges. Phantom pain jabbed at my brain, as if I'd been struck by the bullet. If I could get above treeline, well above treeline, I would be able to escape the possibility of a hunter's bullet finding me instead of a deer. I wondered what other animals, if any, had taken this exact escape route. Bear? Fox? I remembered the previous winter, skiing up Rock Creek Canyon in the eastern Sierra, how I'd followed coyote tracks for miles and wondered then why the coyote was going above treeline in the winter. When I made camp at a frozen lake below the highest peaks, I could see the coyote tracks continuing right up to a pass on the Sierra crest. Visiting family in the valley on the other side? Just loved the view?

As I hunkered up that rocky trail toward Boulder Lake, shouldering my unevenly packed load, exhaustion finally slowing me down, it began to dawn on me that I was acting irrationally. I'd felt that gunshot far too deeply. I knew that although deer hunters did occasionally kill backpackers, the odds were on a par with being struck by lightning. I also knew that the danger of Russell and his friends was negligible. Yet this awareness didn't take away my need to climb, to escape feeling hunted. I moved up, rejoicing in each inch of altitude gained. My legs, though tired, had a will of their own springing from rock to rock. I felt bathed, cleansed by the sweat running off my head and down my neck. I took comfort in knowing that I carried everything I could ever need on my back. The trail petered out at treeline and still I climbed, grabbing the last scrubby spruce for handholds, hungering for the clean, rocky basin I could see still far above me.

I arrived at dusk, my head bursting with exertion and relief. Boulder Lake sat in a barren bowl, circled by the steep walls of blackening mountains. One lone snag, as gray as the granite, leaned out over the water. I set up camp on a tiny ledge above the snag. A perfect patch of sand would cushion my night. There wasn't another person in sight.

My relief was total. Here was rock and water and one stark snag. The dusky sky twitched occasionally, and I had to look hard to make out the flap of wings before they disappeared, like the coyote tracks, to even higher elevations. As darkness wrapped around me, I let all my fear and anxiety drain away. The power of these huge rocks was absolute, as was the cold blackness of the impending night.

I didn't put up my tent. Nor did I sleep much or even think much. I lay in my toasty sleeping bag on the pad of sand and looked up at the stars. Here above treeline, I was nothing more than sweat and iron, muscle and bone, blue and gray, silence and song. Nothing more and nothing less.

At dawn, I watched the sky gray over. The last few stars tickled my eyes, then vanished. I knew it would be a couple of hours before sunrise. I lay very still and watched it arrive, second by second.

Reconnaissance

The air in the desert is like hot breath, menacing and demanding in the way it is all over you, all around you. You have no choice but to give in, let it have your skin. We lay naked, belly up, on top of the cotton blanket, a good couple of feet between us, our legs and arms spread to allow the air, which hadn't cooled a bit since the sun dropped below the horizon, to bathe our bodies. So much dried sweat from the long hot day covered my skin I was a regular salt lick . . . an uncomfortable thought. Who knew what night creatures would emerge to feast on any juicy snacks they could find? The immensity of the desert, and the company of an entire ecosystem of creatures and life forms that have adapted brilliantly, made me feel like a sacrifice. As a pale, water-dependent creature—with nothing protecting my life from this hot sand, this dry wind, the unrelenting sun but a thin furless skin—I was fodder. Especially at night when the desert comes alive.

As if mental exercises could ward off the nighttime army of scavengers and blood-suckers, as if marking myself geographically would offer proof of my existence, maybe hedge against my disappearance, I placed myself. The immediate boundaries of this desert were comforting enough. To the north, water. A fat, wet aqueduct twisted like a snake moving west and away from its source, the Colorado River. To my east, the Chocolate Mountains, hardly intimidating with their edible name. The coast ranges to the west conjured everything the desert was not: soggy, dense, dark green foliage. Finally to my south, the Mexican border, music, tequila, bright colors. This was the Colorado Desert, a region two thousand square miles huge, located in southeastern California. Was it comforting to think of this desert as small compared to its neighbor to the north, the formidable Mojave? No. Any desert too big to escape on foot is boundless.

I struggled to my feet, walked on sand as fine as pastry flour, soothing to my scorched soles, and opened the cooler. I found the big plastic jug of lotion. The lotion smelled like gardenias, lush and green, as I squeezed an enormous mound of it into my palm. I began with my ankles and moved up, palming the cool creaminess into my skin. Finished, I stood and let the whisper of a breeze dry me. I applied another layer.

What next? I looked at Pat lying tangled on the blanket and lay back down beside her. Though it was a moonless night, I could see the black immensity of the mountains behind our camp. In the other direction, at a greater distance, were more mountains, but from here on my back I saw only the immediate ones and the stars emerging in the violet sky. How foolish to go against nature like this. Why was I trying to sleep at the time all desert natives knew to come awake, scavenge, commune, eat, and love? My brain cells, which had slowed to a state of involuntary meditation during the heat of the day, were bursting to life, one by one, like the stars overhead. Like the creatures emerging from their sand tunnels and plant cabanas. Adapting, as if evolving into a desert animal in a matter of minutes, I too began to revive as the night came on.

A trace of coolness in the air. At last. The desert at night is even fresh.

I rolled to my side, the movement of my body making a tiny breeze, and whispered, "You still awake?" I reached out and touched a thigh. Ran my hand up to her waist. Her skin was dry, papery. No answer. How does it happen that the more years you spend with a person the lonelier you feel? It has something to do with the impossibility of being known, really seen and heard, in the way you long to be known, seen and heard. So that the more years you put in with a person, even as a deep kind of comfort develops and passion endures, the more you feel devastatingly alone, alienated.

Three stars shot across the sky, beacons or messengers, beckoning or delivering. Hard to say. Pat stirred, groaned, asked for a Coke.

I rose again and got two Cokes from the cooler, relieved that she'd awakened. I brought the bottle of lotion too.

"I was never asleep," she said. "Just trying. It's noisy out here."

"Yes." Skittering, scratching, even sighing.

I handed her the drink, then got our short chairs. We draped towels over the plastic, then sat, drinking. The agave next to me had knife-like leaves folded over except for one whose sharp point tapped my shoulder. It almost hurt, but I didn't move because it reminded me I was there. An eight-foot stem shot from the center of the plant, looking exactly like a giant asparagus stalk pointing at the stars. The native Cahuillas used the agave for food, but also for tattoo dye.

We had arrived in the desert early that morning, planning to stay a few days, as long as we could hold out, visiting the desert blooms. It was March, much hotter than most Marches, and heavy rains had fallen the previous week causing flash floods in the canyons. The flowers were phenomenal.

"Is this a safe place to camp?" Pat asked now for the first time. During the day it had been too hot to ask questions. We'd driven the truck off the paved highway and up a dirt road until the dirt road withered to a path. We parked and carried our things a bit farther toward the mountains, then camped in the spreading fingers of an arroyo, far from the base of the mountains where it became a canyon, but close enough to discern rivulet paths from the storms last week. She asked a reasonable question. Why would we assume that no rains would fall this week? Would a flash flood be feet or inches deep by the time it reached us?

"No," I answered. "Not really." But we didn't move. After all, though we were sincere about wanting to see the desert blooms, that was only the metaphor for our being here. The flowers were like the top of a mountain, a destination so that you can take the journey. Camping in this wash, planting ourselves in the heart of change, that was our real reason for coming. In spite of its flat, uneventful appearance, no ecosystem is as quickly changeable as the desert. A simple spring downpour can dazzle the grays and reds and browns with the florescence of desert bloom in a matter of hours. Even the shape of the land transforms daily, the winds constantly reshaping the dunes and the floods tearing soil from the arroyos and replacing it in the washes. I came here to feel the immediacy of change, as if I could quicken my capacity to handle it.

I picked up my foot and placed it on hers. My toes caressed the fine bones straining against the skin of her foot, the sand on my sole scratching her. She moved her foot away. We drank more Coke.

Tonight we were mostly silent, but in the daytime we had talked of desert spirituality. Stumbling away from our shade, a bright umbrella plunged deep into the sand, we had hovered over a desert blossom we found fifty yards from camp. Hot pink petals on the flat beavertail cactus. Beside it, a barrel cactus shimmered with crowns of yellow flowers. And all around, like ghosts, the ocotillos growing from the sand like heat waves. Soon, overwhelmed by the sun, even though we were dressed like sheiks in our layers of white cotton, we staggered back to the shade, such as it was, and pulled more cold drinks from the cooler, opened our clothing and rolled the bottles over our thighs, our foreheads, our necks. Replaced them, found colder ones, peeled off the tops and threw back our heads. Drank. Talked some more. If you could call it talking. Out here conversations minimize.

"That flower."

"I never knew fuchsia before."

"You could drink it."

"Yes."

"Breathe it."

"Yes. Taste it."

Then I did. I got up again and walked to a beavertail cactus. Like a mule deer I stretched out my neck, leaned down and pulled part of a bloom off with my lips. It tasted like flower petal, satin fuchsia.

And somehow I felt as if I'd seen god. It's the heat. It's the slight anxiety over creatures you don't understand. A slivering in the sand nearby. A scuttling across your foot. Sometimes when the anxiety brightened for a moment into fear, I considered locking myself in the truck, locking myself against the reptiles and crustaceans and rodents that thrive here. But if I did that I would die of heat. Better to chance contact with the desert fauna. And to endure the current of risk, slight and subtle but present enough to remind me of my vulnerability, and of someone else's authority.

We finished our Cokes and I offered to lotion Pat. She agreed. I started with her shoulders, spent a long time moving down her arms and massaging her fingers with the lotion that smelled like gardenias. I couldn't do her feet because the sand grit scraped painfully.

We laughed and she suggested a walk.

I felt a bolt of dismay at the idea of leaving camp. I glanced at the square of blanket snarled in the sand, then at the truck in the near distance. We had designated this agave, these ocotillos surrounding our camp in their particular pattern, as home, but the spot was truly no safer than any other part of the desert around us. We put on flip-flops to protect our feet against thorns and headed into the desert. The silver chollas looked luminescent, their spines glistening like starlight, like mist. Earlier, in the daylight, I had put my nose in one of the silver cholla's blossoms, the color of unripe apples, sour green with a reddish tint along the outer edges of the petals. Above us the stars looked both hot like dry ice and cold like the blue roots of flame. Nowhere else am I more aware that I am staring into not just the sky but the universe.

"It's a trip out here," I said inanely, wanting only to break the spell of silence.

Naked like me, except for flip-flops, Pat didn't even turn her head, as if my words had been swallowed by the bigness before they could travel the few inches to her ear. I looked behind us. I could no longer see our blanket but the truck stood out like a dark tank, out of place and useless. And getting smaller as we walked on. I began to wonder why we were walking.

"Because we can't walk in the day," she explained. "It's awesome. Look."

I did look and it was awesome, but the space was beginning to feel too big. It pressed in on me like it had the intensified gravity of a black hole. I loved the wilderness for reminding me of my place in the wider realm, for reducing my fears to biological reasonability, but out here the ratio was too exaggerated. I felt on the brink of being squeezed to absolute nothingness. I wanted to touch Pat, to know my flesh by traveling hers.

She walked a distance away from me, maintaining the gap when I tried to close it, moving as if I were the repellant end of a magnet. Maybe she was reveling in the loneliness.

I grabbed a handful of sand, sifted it through my fingers, kept walking.

"Look." She finally moved to me, touched my shoulder.

I looked to the mountains, not the ones buttressing our camp but the ones in the other direction, in the distance. "What?"

"Do you see that light?"

I scanned the night sky, now looking away from the mountains and toward the expanse of desert, and saw an odd white light with yellowish tinges. It bobbed gently as it moved slowly in a path perpendicular to ours.

"A single headlight," I said. "We're probably getting closer to the highway. Some car with one headlight out."

"No. Too high in the sky."

Soon I realized there was a second light behind it, then a third. A string of seven lights, all bobbing gently in the night sky, at least a mile or two away, moving slowly in single file like a family of ducks.

I was pleased to have a mystery to solve, a topic of conversation, something to engage my attention other than the vastness. I studied the lights, wondering. I've spent many nights in the outdoors, and I've seen a lot of strange stuff in the sky, and none of it has ever frightened me. Most of it I have assumed to be satellites.

These were no satellites. They were far too low in the sky. Nor were they airplanes or any other craft with an engine, for they were absolutely silent.

I racked my brain for explanations.

Of course I knew what my friends would say, what would be "obvious" to anyone to whom I described this experience: the military. The desert is known to be a playground for bomb testing and other military maneuvers. A couple of years earlier, I'd spent an entire backpack trip diving for cover as the sky exploded time and again. Later I learned that they were researching the sound barrier and the multiple explosions were sonic booms.

So I tried to look at my bobbing lights as a military experiment. But in this age of supersonic jets and space shuttles, softly bobbing lights are hard to explain. They were perfectly silent. They moved slowly, deliberately. Weather or surveillance balloons were possible, but why at night? Why over the state park? We were a long way away from the Nevada border and the larger deserts where military experiments were common.

My mind, charged by adrenaline, ran through and rejected all the possibilities, which made these lights, by definition, bona fide UFOs, as in flying objects I could not identify. I saw my face in blurry lurid colors splashed across a tabloid, along with my claim. *Science writer sights UFO.* But then I reminded myself that it was not only the tabloids that reported on UFOs. Since the beginning of time, very respectable publications and people had described inexplicable phenomena in the sky. Even biblical stories have been interpreted as UFO sightings, such as the prophet Ezekiel who reported seeing a fire-spitting, gleaming bronze craft from which four living creatures emerged. And what about Alexander the Great, who claimed that he and his army had been harassed by a pair of flying objects?

So I was in the company of prophets and world conquerors. Somehow that was more disturbing than comforting. As the bobbing lights drew closer, I reined in my imagination and forced myself to think harder about possible natural explanations.

But none of the usual natural explanations fit the present situation. All the literature on UFOs that explained away sightings as atmospheric abnormalities used examples that were obvious: People reported shooting stars, Venus on nights it was particularly bright, strange reflections of the sun, even the reflection of a camera lens on window glass. The lights approaching me were not reflections of anything, nor were they misidentified heavenly bodies. They were too low in the sky; I could see the dark backdrop of the mountains behind them. Most of all, it was the *way* they moved that began to truly unnerve me.

The string of seven lights, bobbing ever so slightly in the night sky, changed their course. They had been moving in a line perpendicular to us, toward the mountain range in the distance. As we stood and watched, utterly naked save for the flip-flops, the lead light turned slowly, imperceptibly at first but by now decidedly, and headed directly for us. There was something else: I had the sense, the strong sense, as did Pat when we talked about it later, that these bobbing lights were guided by intelligence. They headed for us, as if to sniff us as an animal would do, moving neither randomly nor by a prearranged pattern or blueprint—without precision and *with* decided will. They seemed curious.

As they approached us, my fear intensified. In fact, this situation was quickly becoming one of the scariest in my life. Scarier than the time I developed hypothermia after falling through ice into a stream in New Hampshire's winter wilderness. Scarier than the time I clung to the edge of a crumbling cliff, looking down hundreds of feet below me. Scarier, too, than the time I stood alone for the first time in my new room after leaving home at eighteen. While experiencing these earlier fears, I somehow had remained engaged. I had known I couldn't indulge the fear because I had to act. This time the fear was stripped to its essence. This time there was no action to be taken. The seven bobbing lights were approaching, dipping lower in the sky as if to get a better look at me and Pat. Yes, I admit I did go so far as to imagine a spacecraft landing, a hatch opening, and little beings waddling toward me. Pointing. Laughing. Forcing me into their spacecraft. Explaining in perfect English, or in garbled alienese, that they wanted me for science experiments, or worse, on their planet.

I did imagine abduction. In detail. And for those moments this science writer truly believed it was possible.

Begging Pat to come with me, I began to run. Where do you run to in the desert? There was nowhere to go but back to camp. At least that was a home of sorts and I needed to get there. As I ran, panting,

I looked over my shoulder. The lights kept coming, bobbing, taking their time, while I, an exposed bundle of human cells, ran through the desert night. I quit looking over my shoulder and just ran.

In hindsight, I'm glad she tackled me, though if I'd been a few years older I'm sure she would have induced a heart attack. My scream seared the cooling desert air. The impact of her body knocked me face first in the sand, silencing the scream and restructuring my fear. Like the way an injection of energy can transform the molecular structure of a substance, the skeleton of my fear, though still fear, took on a powerful erotic charge. I was grateful for the length of my body against the Earth. And for the length of her body against mine.

She apologized for the attack from behind.

"Don't move," I said.

It was not, she explained, that she was any less scared than me, but her fear had taken another form. My running terrified her, made her feel we'd provoke a chase, like running from a bear.

And so there I lay, as close to my partner, my home, my life, as I'd ever be, and yet I still confronted the alone of me, and even worse, the idea of myself as prey. I thought of the word alien, as in alienation, the opposite of what I longed for in wilderness.

We lay in the sand together, our bodies wet and gritty with perspiration plus sand, our hard breathing the only sound for miles. The lights, still in a line, oscillated in the not-far distance but seemed to have stopped their approach. As if they'd seen enough of these pitiful Earth creatures, they turned, again imperceptibly at first, and headed for the mountain range. We watched them retreat, voyeurs to the aliens, their menace feeding the passion of the desert. Eventually, the first light rose slightly and skimmed over the peaks, then dropped behind the mountains, out of sight. The rest of the lights followed, one by one, each rising to miss the peaks and disappearing behind the range. Then, feeling equally foolish and anointed, somehow favored, we talked eagerly, the human voice an oasis. We tried to imagine the bobbing lights being piloted by American soldiers in green camouflage suits, running surveillance or tests or simply joyriding in some new, or not-so-new, toys. With the military, we agreed, anything was possible.

But that was just the point: anything *was* possible. And as we talked, the military explanation seemed just a wee bit more absurd than other possibilities. The idea that only this one planet, only this one speck in the universe, sponsors intelligence is illogical. Think of the ant making a journey across Pat's hip as we lay in the desert sand. I'm sure that it, along with all its comrade ants, perceived itself to be the top rung in the order of things, entirely oblivious to the existence of humans and most other species, even though by some remote chance this one was traversing a human body as we spoke. Isn't it possible, even likely, that we are the ants to other forms of life or intelligence in the universe? Couldn't we be just as oblivious?

Pat brushed away the ant and got up. She weaved her fingers among the thorns of a nearby succulent and tore a fat leaf from the plant. She broke off one of the thorns and used it to trace a tattoo on my breast. Then she dug her fingernails into the flesh of the leaf, accidentally piercing her palm with a thorn. Still, she continued until she managed to break the rubbery flesh. A clear gel oozed out. She scooped a fingerful and applied it to my skin, cool and slippery.

As I relinquished myself to her hands, I realized that all of us—the bobbing lights, whether military or alien, the ant traveling the landscape of Pat's body, and even I—were on reconnaissance missions. Hadn't I come to the desert to watch, to see, to measure myself against what I found here? We are nothing but this watchfulness, this constant reconnaissance in the hopes of finding fertile geography on which to feast, whether that geography be a piece of fruit, a person, a desert, a planet. What matters is the simultaneous feast, being laid bare, the sand in your crevices, the sting of the agave leaf, the tattoo needle or starlight, the place where your flesh intersects another geography. I closed my eyes to better concentrate on the sand scraping against my back, the something sharp—a piece of rock or a thorn—digging into my hip. In my left ear I heard the tiny clatter of a hard-shelled animal and on my skin I felt the balm of cactus pulp.

How to Prey

Y OU ARE ENTERING MOUNTAIN LION HABITAT. I stopped in front of the sign, which was affixed to a metal roadside pole, and stared at the blue stencil of a mountain lion, its long tail seeming to swish back and forth territorially. I had just cycled up residential Grizzly Peak Boulevard toward Tilden Regional Park, the urban wilderness capping the East Bay hills, and was now stopped next to Berkeley's Space Sciences Laboratory where internationally renowned physicists probed the heart, or many hearts, of the universe. Sheepishly, I recalled my run from space aliens in the Colorado Desert. But here, right now, announced on this sign, was a true predator. Urban mountain lions.

I'd heard of the big cats in the dry, rolling grasslands southeast of the bay, but in Berkeley? When had this sign gone up? I'd been cycling here for years, riding up through the neighborhoods until I reached the parks on the crest of the ridge, happy to get a breather from the city but knowing that the city was always nearby. Indeed, San Francisco and the Golden Gate Bridge hovered like Oz on the horizon of my view as I pedaled. I had assumed that the animals, the big ones, the grizzlies of Grizzly Peak Boulevard, for example, had long disappeared. Sure there are deer, and occasionally I spot a coyote. But mountain lions? Top of the food chain carnivorous predators? Eight-foot-long cats?

YOU ARE ENTERING MOUNTAIN LION HABITAT, the sign read. And then in smaller print: "Warn mountain lions of your presence—sing, whistle, or talk as you hike. Adult mountain lions can be up to eight feet long, tawny colored, black-tipped ears and tail. Mountain lions are unpredictable and have been known to attack without warning."

At the bottom of the sign it said, "In an emergency call 911."

I could just see it. I'm hiking along a fire trail and a mountain lion pounces. I whip out my cell phone, punch 911, and tell the dispatcher that I'm in Tilden Park fighting off a very large cat. Please rush.

The absurdity of calling 911 aside, I was transfixed by this sign. It was as if a tiny bit of the wild, a vestige of a grand adventure, had slipped through the cracks of the mundane routine of my daily life. I wanted to see one. That desire instantly became resolve: I would *look* for the mountain lion.

In a big and sudden shift, I shed my feelings of being prey—from the bobbing lights in the Colorado Desert, the deer hunters' gunshot in the Trinity Alps, the stalking mountain goat, to even the phantom husband of Barbara in the Mojave. Forget being on the run. Where were those mountain lions and what was their predatory secret?

The next day as I rode my bicycle up Grizzly Peak, I scrutinized the brush on either side of the road, looking for two yellow eyes, the flick of a black-tipped tail, the twitch of giant whiskers. As if the cats would be strolling in broad daylight along the roadside jogger's path. Instead, I spotted a park ranger. As she turned her pale green pickup truck onto a gravel pullout, I flagged her down.

"What about these new mountain lion signs?" I asked.

"There are no mountain lions in Tilden Park. Those signs were put up to be extra safe. Do not worry. I promise you, if there were even the *possibility* of a mountain lion around here, we would close the park so fast you wouldn't know what happened."

"No," I finally managed to get a word in. "I'm not afraid. This is exciting—"

"*Do not worry*," she counseled emphatically. "You are *perfectly* safe."

"But—"

Her eyes were nearly swimming in her determination to comfort me and there was nothing I could do to get her to address anything other than my possible fear.

"Why," I insisted, "would they put up the signs if there were no mountain lions?"

"Extreme caution," she said. "We try to be extremely cautious."

"You don't understand." Something compelled me to persist, perhaps my hope that if she knew my desire, she would let me in on their little feline secret. "I *want* to see a mountain lion. I'm thrilled by the idea of bigger-than-newt wildlife in Tilden."

Now she laughed derisively—a response I would see more of in my pursuit of mountain lions—shook her head, and climbed back in her truck. She thought me a naïve nature-lover. I probably hugged trees, too. Didn't I know that these were killer cats, not kitty cats?

Deflated, I cycled back down the hill and tried to plan the course of my investigation. Were there really mountain lions in Tilden Regional Park, the wilderness crowning the Bay Area sprawl? Or was this just another urban myth? One big bureaucratic base-covering that had nothing to do with real animals, just the fear of animals.

A couple recent memories fueled my curiosity. In the first one, I was on my bike again, flying down the hill, back into the city, when something leapt into my path. A full-grown buck with an enormous rack froze in the middle of Spruce Street and stared at me. Careening, I squeezed the hand brakes as hard as I could. It wasn't hard or fast enough. I would have hit the buck and impaled myself on one of about twelve points if the deer hadn't overcome its paralysis at the last moment and bolted.

Though this was the most magnificent deer I had seen in Berkeley neighborhoods, it was hardly the first. More often during my cycling forays, I passed deer grazing in backyards or along the sides of the roads. The animals looked healthy, and the does were often accompanied by fawns. By all appearances, the deer population was increasing. Mountain lions prey almost exclusively on deer. Could the apparent increase in urban deer be luring the mountain lions?

In the second memory, I was walking at night with a friend down a short, steep road through Tilden Park. As it is every winter, this road was closed to cars in order to protect the endangered newts that cross the pavement with the washes of rain. There was no moon; the night was cold and still. About halfway down the hill, my friend and I heard an odd noise coming from the dense brush alongside the road. It was a keening, much like the sound of a woman crying in intense pain or fear. Yet there were no other sounds of struggle. It definitely wasn't a bird, and clearly the little newt couldn't make that much noise.

What I remember best is how the sound struck something primal in both my friend and me. My heart thudded as we made our way to my car walking backwards, so as not to turn our backs on the human-like cries. What was worse, a rustling in the brush beside the road followed us about half of the way up the hill. This was a *big* rustling. No bird. No fox. Definitely no newt.

At the time, the only possible solution was a person, some crazy person lurking in the bushes and following two terrified women. That seemed highly unlikely. The person would have to be very crazy. Why not spring out onto the road and scare us for real? Why follow along in the dense brush that would be very difficult for a person to navigate? And the keening, what could that have been?

I didn't need to go any farther than the *World Book* to find this: "The cry of the mountain lion is wild and terrifying. It sounds like a woman screaming in pain."

I continued the early stages of my hunt within the safety of the library. I already knew that mountain lions are a solid tawny color (except for the cubs, which are covered with black spots) and their tails are tipped with brown and black. A male weighs between 110 and 180 pounds, a female between 80 and 130 pounds. They eat any game they can catch, but their main prey is deer. For that reason, they need habitat that is rich in deer and dense with cover for hiding and stalking. The males wander a large territory, up to one hundred square miles, while the females prowl around sixty square miles. Incredibly adaptable, they can be found from sea level to over fourteen thousand feet and in the mountains, deserts, and forests. Historically, mountain lions roamed all over the Americas. Today, they live in the twelve western states, in the Canadian provinces of British Columbia and Alberta, and a tiny population still lives in Florida.

Because of the species' wide distribution, mountain lions are known by many names. Cougar comes from the Guarani Indians of Brazil who called them *cuguacuarana*. Puma comes from an Incan language and means "a powerful animal." The Cherokee of the southeastern United States called the big cats *klandagi*, meaning "lord of the forest." The terms cougar, mountain lion, and puma are the most common names used in the western United States, while panther, painter (colloquial for panther), and catamount (for cat-of-the-mountains) are used in the east.

In the last decade of the twentieth century, two human deaths by mountain lion—the first in California in eighty-five years—were pretty strong indicators that our habitats were beginning to once again overlap. In 1994 a marathon runner was training in the wooded foothills of El Dorado County, and a lion pounced on her from behind, knocking her down a hillside. Her spine was broken and her skull crushed. Lion prints were found near the attack and her body was partially eaten. A week later, a team of hounds found a lion in the area, chased it up a tree, and the lion was killed. Its carcass was displayed at a wildlife forensic laboratory in Rancho Cordova in Sacramento County with its paws in brown paper bags to preserve possible evidence under its claws. It was said that the dental pattern of the two-or-three-year-old, eighty-three-pound female matched the neck wounds on the runner. DNA tests subsequently proved that the suspect lion was the killer. Eight months later, in the back-country of San Diego County, a bird watcher was also killed by a mountain lion.

The publicity of mountain lions skyrocketed with these two deaths. Along with the publicity came more sightings, triggering fear and a debate on whether the mountain lions needed—or *deserved*—their protected status.

I felt uneasy as I pored over the newspaper clippings from this post-attack era. On May 1, 1994, the *San Francisco Examiner* ran a story with the headline: "Mountain lions are hardly 'cuddly' kittens." The reporter asserted that the big cats "are powerful, fleet-footed killers that sometimes attack just for sport" and questioned the mountain lions' right to be protected, given their amorality. Not only do they kill people, the reporter warned, mountain lions kill deer. "With jaws strong enough to bite through skulls like great white sharks taking chomps out of surfers' legs, these cats stalk and kill 250,000 deer a year in California."

The hysteria in this journalism doesn't jibe with the facts about mountain lions. Applying human ethics to the behavior of another species is absurd. And hypocritical. The biggest cause of death for mountain lions is the human predator. A minimum of 65,665 cougars were shot, poisoned, trapped, or snared by bounty hunters, federal hunters, and sport hunters from 1907 to 1978 in the twelve western states, British Columbia, and Alberta. That figure does not include unreported mountain lion killings.

Now, which species is it that kills "just for sport"?

In 1990 the Wildlife Protection Act, Proposition 117, banned trophy hunting of mountains lions in California. Known as the Mountain Lion Initiative, the law protects vast acres of wildlife habitat for an array of species, not just mountain lions. It has helped in the recovery of many rare, threatened, and endangered species, such as the bald eagle, the California condor, the chinook salmon, the golden eagle, the greater sandhill crane, the peregrine falcon, the bird-footed checkbloom, the slender-petaled mustard, and the ringtail cat, to name a few. But in 1996, following the two human deaths, the cat's enemies put up Proposition 197, a ballot measure that sought to weaken Proposition 117 and allow lions to be hunted for sport again.

That measure was defeated. But clearly the "mountain lion question" was coming to a dramatic head and the issue was being presented with a curious emotionalism. Are mountain lions "cuddly kittens" or are they "ferocious killers"? As if these were the only two choices. Mountain lions are wild animals; no one would suggest letting them under the covers at night. Like all other species, they get a meal the best way they know how. In fact, the second most common cause of death for mountain lions, next to being killed by humans, is starvation. It is unlikely they are expending a lot of energy killing for kicks.

This emotionalism—kitty cat versus serial killer—is a red herring. But what is the real issue? Why are people so wrought up? I sensed something deeper than the political issue of whether the cats should be protected. What lurked behind the Tilden Park ranger's vehemence about the *absence* of danger? The *San Francisco Examiner* reporter's vehemence about the *presence* of danger? What exactly, I wanted to know, was at stake here?

I guessed that the best way to a mountain lion's heart was through its stomach, so I called up Dale McCullough, a University of California at Berkeley professor who studied deer living in residential neighborhoods. He told me that residential deer were so prevalent that they had been seen on the university campus, at a subway station in Oakland, and crossing a shopping mall in El Cerrito. He'd been tagging deer to find out how they spend their time and why they are moving into our neighborhoods. He wanted to know how deer functioned in the urban setting. Where are they and where do they go? How large an area does an individual deer cover? How are they making a living?

A pest to gardeners, these Bambi-gone-bad deer devour roses, which to them are like ice cream—sweet, high in protein, and delicious. The deer also kick, sometimes killing, pet dogs. McCullough didn't think the deer were being forced out of the wild by drought or any other cause. Rather, they were coming into our neighborhoods because it is great deer habitat. "The best thing for the deer are the serious gardeners."

The problem, according to the professor, is that the deer are becoming quite tame. "Escape and hiding cover is absent down the hill, but now deer have no fear of humans. They are willing to camp on the front porch like the family dog."

So what does this have to do with the mountain lions?

"It seems beyond any stretch of the imagination that there are more mountain lions now than in any time in California history. We have lots of deer." McCullough added, "Mountain lions are deer-killing machines." He warned, "With more mountain lions come other kinds of problems such as attacks on humans. And they take the most vulnerable—fawns, children, small women. These attacks are violent encounters. Mountain lions who can get a meal without risking a lot are going to take it. It's perfectly predictable that there are going to be attacks in urban areas and then we'll find out what the tolerance is for mountain lions."

I asked about our encroachment on their habitat, and he answered, "We're moving out, but they're invading us. Just like the deer: we're moving into their habitat but they are also moving toward us."

It sounded like war. Something from which we needed to protect women and children.

McCullough said that the next "obvious step in this progression" was that a child was going to get attacked. "The media is going to have a real feeding frenzy when a young child gets attacked in our urban area. It's going to be a horrendous time."

"This isn't mysterious," McCullough kept repeating. "It's common sense."

In conclusion, he stated, "It's all what society wants for the animals."

Wandering back across the campus to my car, I wondered. Is it really? Are we—society—in control?

It's the job of the Department of Fish and Game to control—well, *manage*—wildlife for society, and so, following the professor's lead, I gave them a call next. When Lieutenant Miles Young returned my call, he stated the time in military hours and used his rank in referring to himself, giving me the impression, yet again, that what we were engaged in here with the big cats was nothing short of war. The lieutenant told me, "I've lived here for twenty-seven years. You see more snakes, gophers, deer. How come? More houses and less land for the animals. It doesn't take a rocket scientist to see why there are more mountain lions."

Young warned that we "need to keep them culled." He said that "we now have three generations of lions that haven't been hunted. Now cubs don't have fear of humans." Like the professor, Young foresaw impending disaster. With the allegedly increasing mountain lion population, decreasing habitat, and increasing fodder, something was going to happen.

Young thought the mountain lions needed to be studied, not the deer. Of McCullough's study, he said, "Why would you spend thousands of dollars studying deer? Why is he doing this?" The deer, he said, were doing exactly what you would expect. "They could have used the same amount of money for tracking devices on mountain lions." He added, "I'm just a dumb cop out here and I don't understand what they are doing." No one, he claimed, wanted to fund a mountain lion study. Why? Because they would have to do something. "What if they came up with a study that confirmed eight mountain lions? People would freak."

I hung up the phone beginning to feel as if I were in a Nevada Barr novel, stepping deeper and deeper into an environmental mystery like some kind of "dumb cop" myself. I got little information from Lieutenant Young, a whole lot more speculation, and more of that inflated emotionalism. What was this buzz beneath everyone's mountain lion story? *It doesn't take a rocket scientist. It's all common sense. There's no mystery here.* You could have fooled me.

I reviewed the facts (as Barr's ranger sleuth is fond of doing): two human deaths, lots of deer, a couple of ballot initiatives.* Meanwhile, as much time as I spent in the urban wilderness on the crest of the East Bay hills, I'd seen neither hide nor hair of this beast that was omnipresent in so many people's minds.

Time to get out of the library and off the phone.

Early one morning I drove about forty miles southeast to Sunol Regional Park, where there had been several confirmed sightings of mountain lions. The interpretive ranger at Sunol showed none of the paranoia of my earlier contacts, perhaps because she spent her days in the field with the lions and understood my hopes of seeing one. She suggested I hike out to Little Yosemite where they had been most recently sighted.

*In 2004, after a hiatus of ten years, a mountain lion attack resulted in a third California fatality.

Taking the hills route, I started out across tall golden grasses, all too aware that they were the exact color of a cougar's coat. Twice in recent years Sunol had been closed because of mountain lions wandering into the camping areas. I could easily see why they were at home strolling across these hot hillsides and finding shade in the pockets of live oaks nestled into the valleys. Right away I saw two blacktail deer grazing on a far hillside and wondered what their rate of success was in evading the mountain lion. Red-tailed hawks circled overhead, keeping the concept of "predator" fresh in my mind. I walked as erect as possible so that no mistake could be made between me and a four-legged grazer. Already I had ignored the first recommendation by the Department of Fish and Game on how to avoid mountain lion encounters: do not hike alone. Of course, my goal was not to avoid the lions, but I did want to avoid interacting with one.

I stood still for a moment among the tall grasses and thought of my childhood fantasies of finding a home in the wild, my interest in edible plants, as well as in caves and thickets and other natural shelters. In other words, my animal interest in food and cover. All living things feast and are feasted upon, and that explains just about everything. Just about. Certainly the fear. And also desire. But what about this hunt of mine right now, my need to see a mountain lion, a pursuit that wouldn't win me food or shelter? Would not, to think in terms of biological evolution, win a single thing for the continuation of my own DNA or my species. And yet, there was still something feral about my mountain lion hunt, this giant U-turn I was making from prey to predator. I wanted something from the mountain lion.

It was early summer and there were plenty of California poppies, mustard, and once I descended toward Alameda Creek, a few lupines. Little Yosemite is ambitiously named: boulders line a sweet creek that, while not anything majestic like the real Yosemite, is a surprising delight in such a dry, hot park. Alder, willow, and sycamore shade the pools and lots of private nooks along the creek.

I found the biggest pool at the top of Little Yosemite deserted and sat down on the pebble beach to wait for my lion. I felt more than a little foolish. Most rangers, game wardens, and other wildlife specialists had laughed or even scoffed when I'd asked where I might be most likely to see a mountain lion. They thought I didn't know how slim the odds were. They thought I was a tree-hugger who expected to be able to pet one of the big cats. I didn't really blame them. Both Fish and Game and the Regional Parks received endless false reports of mountain lion sightings. Each sighting had to be taken seriously, and tax dollars were spent investigating, usually only to find anything from large house cats to red setters.

My own mountain lion investigation helped me understand their weariness. A few days earlier a friend who knew I was on the hunt had called me, breathlessly leaving a message that she'd heard on the radio that a mountain lion had been struck by a car on College Avenue. I immediately started calling media sources, trying to find out if anyone knew anything about the mountain lion that had been hit by a car on a commercial street in Berkeley. And so a rumor began.

The mountain lion, I found out about eight calls later, had been struck on College Avenue in the smaller, much more rural town of Santa Rosa.

In fact, I began getting calls regularly from helpful friends reporting on sightings. These reports were never firsthand, always from a friend of a friend who'd seen the cat. A few phone calls later I'd find out that the friend had read about a lion in the newspaper or had seen one of the very signs that had kindled *my* initial interest. Once a woman told me that her son had seen a mountain lion on a Berkeley school playground. It turned out to be true. A zoologist had brought several big cats in captivity for the children to view.

That my friends were intrigued enough in what I was doing to tell *their* friends about my search only confirmed my observation that people are very, *very* interested in mountain lions. That's why I didn't regret tracking down these false reports. They revealed how the mere existence of mountain lions triggers something deep inside of us. People see them everywhere, even where they are not. I even started to dream about them. In my dreams they strolled about in perfect, domineering splendor. I had never seen a mountain lion, and yet my unconscious could picture it in full, perfect detail. Why? What is it about these cats that holds our attention absolutely? Why is the mascot for every other small-town high school a cougar? Why had the recent attacks, which could be counted on the fingers of one hand, brought us to alert so much more quickly than a ridiculously higher number of fatal car accidents? No one was lobbying for legislation to take cars out of our urban areas.

Why, for that matter, was I so eager to see a mountain lion in the flesh?

As I sat on the pebble beach at Little Yosemite, I kept glancing up at a stone ledge hanging out toward the pool of water, well over my head, imagining that if a cat did appear, that was where it would enter. Above me. Poised on a ledge, surveying the lay of the creek, supreme.

Late afternoon light danced with shadows on the green and purple boulders surrounding the pool. The air turned silvery with evening. As the sun went down, the stones became dark reflections in the pool, disturbed only by ripples made by an evening breeze.

The cat never appeared though I stayed until well after dusk. Walking back the road route, I nearly stepped on the biggest spider I have ever seen in my life. The tarantula was a couple of inches across and as furry as a mammal. Its hinged legs moved in the most amazing, unsynchronized way, and I thought, as I have so many times, how in nature the pursuit of one goal almost always leads to another kind of discovery. I crouched down and watched the tarantula for a long time. But I still wanted to see a mountain lion. I didn't care if the odds were a thousand to one, I would keep trying.

The second time I drove out to Sunol, leaving in the late afternoon to try to catch a lion at dusk, I inched along in the traffic leaving the urban congestion. Entering the dry hills of the southeastern East Bay, I passed one housing development after another, and then, before the highway broke free into open country, I passed the half-built new developments that seemed to be always pushing out the edges of the city. California's human population skyrocketed from 9.6 million in 1945 to 34 million in 2000 (at the last census and still climbing), and people need space. They need homes. Habitat. According to the Mountain Lion Foundation newsletter, every single day at least 150 acres of mountain lion habitat are lost forever to bulldozers, asphalt, and concrete.

It doesn't take a rocket scientist, after all. This is a struggle for habitat—between humans and cougars. Obviously, it is we who are moving into their backyard and not the other way around. No one would argue with the fact that they were here first. And where are they to go now?

Mountain lion populations are always sparse in comparison to populations of most other animals because of their need for very large territories and their position at the top of the food chain. Many mountain lion kittens don't survive into adulthood, but those that do must eventually find territory of their own. It is these adolescents, roving in search of their own territories, that get into trouble with humans.

Young cougars leave their mothers at between twelve and eighteen months of age. Called transients, they wander about, often covering great distances, sometimes for as long as a year, in search of food and a home range. The lions are very vulnerable at this stage in their lives because they are moving through unfamiliar terrain, have not yet honed their hunting skills, and are prone to wander into human habitat. Transients are more likely than older cats to attack livestock, pets, or humans. Not too savvy yet, they are looking for opportunities, sometimes making big mistakes—a lot like adolescents of our own species.

As the state's human population soars, and more and more prime mountain lion habitat is turned into suburban backyards, human-cougar encounters are bound to happen with increasing frequency. And yet, some people who leave the city to live in outlying areas seem to expect the wildlife, whose habitat they have overtaken, to live by human rules. Leaving the city, by definition, means entering the wild. Do people really believe that the gates to their housing developments can shut out all but the big blue sky?

All creatures, including people, want safe homes. The absence of predators. But in these situations, just who exactly is the predator and who is the prey?

I spent another lazy evening in Sunol Regional Park but I didn't find any cats.

The more I read and talked to people about California's mountain lions, the more I realized that for most people the central question was: how many of them are there? Are these beasts lurking in great numbers in the hills, fat and happy, reproducing quickly, with time on their paws to hunt for sport? Or are they lean, barely existing, frightened of the humans encroaching on their habitat? Mountain lions are so elusive that no one really knew. But everyone did know that the answer would dictate the future of human relationships with the lions.

Steve Bobzien, a wildlife resource analyst for the East Bay Regional Parks, kept a database of sightings and incidents, recording only the ones that had merit. He said that sightings came in cycles and sometimes he'd receive a few in quick succession and then none for weeks or even months. The majority of sightings were casual, brief observations, a minute at the most in duration. Bobzien took a cautious approach to answering my questions, clearly not wanting to alienate anyone on either side of the issue, reinforcing my perception of a controversy deeper than the political one. While a mountain lion supporter himself, he urged sensitivity toward people's fear of the big cats, calling them, "instinctive baseline feelings of fear." He confirmed that no one really knew if the mountain lion population was growing, that there was no solid data. He pointed out that increased reported sightings did not necessarily mean more lions. The publicity from the deaths and the ballot initiatives put the cougars in the front of people's minds. Maybe people had seen lions in the past but hadn't called anyone to report the sightings. Also, the fact that we're moving into mountain lion habitats might mean that people are seeing the lions more but not necessarily that there are more lions.

Shawn Smallwood, an independent mountain lion expert who did his doctorate work on mountain lions at University of California at Davis, contended that one man knows how many mountain lions are in California and he's that man. Working for himself, Smallwood conducted a statewide track count. He counted track sets and monitored the mountain lion population in California from 1985 until 1995. "I have the best guess," he said, and it's around 1,100 mountain lions, which is about five thousand less than the number Fish and Game claims for the state. About this discrepancy, Smallwood said, "Very much their motivation is to have jurisdiction over mountain lion hunting. I don't trust their numbers or motivation."

According to Smallwood, there are communities that *want* a mountain lion nearby. In his travels, he has encountered several park officials and community leaders who have asked if he could get them a mountain lion. Why? To thin problematic and overgrown deer herds.

Deer, as it turns out, are more dangerous and have taken many more human lives than mountain lions ever have. Nationwide, over the last one hundred years, ten thousand people have been killed by deer. Fifteen thousand have been killed by lightning. Even bees cause many more human deaths than mountain lions—four thousand deaths by bee sting over the last one hundred years. In this time period, only fourteen fatal cougar attacks have occurred on the entire North American continent. Each *year* domestic dogs kill eighteen to twenty people and inflict two hundred thousand injuries requiring stitches. Even jellyfish and spiders account for more human deaths per year than mountain lions.

So why are some people so eager to prove that the cougar population is big and growing, so desperate to "cull" the lions, so afraid of their existence?

I asked Lynn Sadler, the director of the Mountain Lion Foundation, if she thought the California mountain lion population was growing. She explained that mountain lions kill one another for territory. As a population, they do not allow overgrowth. It's possible, she said, that you'd see a brief surge in a population but not a growth spurt that lasts very long. They regulate themselves.

So what motivation would Fish and Game have for inflating their estimation of the mountain lion population, if indeed they did? Sadler said that Fish and Game gets a lot of funding from hunting licenses. She also explained that the hunting of mountain lions is promoted by clubs, such as the Safari Club, whose members set goals of killing an individual from each of several big game categories. Mountain lion protectors are messing with these hunters' desire to complete their collections. Sadler added, "Then there are the real sickos who think that if you can get the last of a species, you are really doing well."

Hunting mountain lions is hard work. It requires tremendous patience, stealth, and usually a team of hounds. Few people are capable of doing it on their own. Many hunters hire guides. According to Kevin Hansen, author of *Cougar: The American Lion*, "While most hunting guides run legitimate operations, the expense of long pursuits and the impatience of clients to bag a trophy cat entice some guides to provide a higher level of convenience in the form of 'will-call' (as in, 'When we have your cougar treed, we will call you') or 'shootout' (as in, 'All you have to do is shoot it out of the tree') hunts. The guide puts a list of clients in his pocket, then heads out into the woods to find and track a cougar." Once he has the cat treed he calls the client to come get it.

It gets worse. Some people will do anything to shoot a cat. On November 16, 1990, state and federal authorities raided Dawn and Floyd Patterson's ranch near Lockwood, California. They found skulls, heads, and hides of mountain lions, Bengal tigers, spotted leopards, black leopards, and jaguars. The animals were believed to be surplus zoo animals. The Pattersons charged "big game hunters" up to $3,500 for the opportunity to kill a cat—often right in the stock trailer. The "hunters" got to keep the carcasses to stuff and, presumably, display at home. The Pattersons were tried and convicted on forty-two counts of violating state wildlife laws.

Cougars have been also killed for the hefty cash their gallbladders bring. A bear's gallbladder, which is considered to have healing powers in other parts of the world, is worth $7,000 to $10,000. A mountain lion's gallbladder looks almost identical to that of a bear.

People can be pretty vicious animals. No news there, really. What was becoming clear, though, was that this wasn't a political issue: it was a biological one. A matter of predation. Who was going to kill whom?

I learned about a fresh kill out at Lake Chabot, a park just south of Oakland, and this time the mountain lion incident wasn't just a rumor. Three deer carcasses had been discovered. Steve Bobzien had investigated the deer himself and confirmed that they looked very much like the work of a mountain lion. The carcasses, he surmised, were discovered immediately after the kill. There were drag marks where the lion (or lions) had tried to carry off the carcasses before abandoning them. Usually cats bury their prey to keep it hidden and fresh for future feedings, but Bobzien explained that they were probably interrupted in their feasts and were forced to leave the deer carcasses covered with only a few leaves. It was obvious, he said, that these deer were killed by cats, not coyotes. Dogs attack from the hindquarters and are extremely messy killers. A cougar, on the other hand, is an extremely neat killer. It bites the back of the neck, severing the spinal cord and causing almost immediate death. The cat then plucks the fur from the point of incision with its teeth. Using its sharp claws, it opens the flank behind the ribs. The stomach and intestines are pulled out and dragged away from the carcass. Then the heart and liver are removed and eaten first. If it's been a long time since the cougar has eaten, it will eat up to ten pounds of meat. Then it will bury the carcass for future gorging.

Off I went to Lake Chabot, hoping to run into the killer. I began walking the trail that circumnavigates the large lake, listening to noises in the undergrowth, wishing I possessed the more attuned senses of other animals. When I'd gone far enough to leave other hikers behind, I stretched myself out catlike on a rock next to the water. A beam of sun shot through the canopy of trees, warming my body. Though I felt a bit like a human offering, laid out on a prominent stone next to a sacred body of water, I didn't intend myself to be bait. But it was hard not to consider the possibility of being prey. Truly, it wasn't that scary of a prospect. Death by mountain lion—a quick lethal bite—seemed much less frightening than, for just one example, a slow and painful death by cancer. Maybe there would be one feral moment of recognition, *intense* recognition, when my head whipped around and saw the mountain lion going for the back of my neck, that my death would be the purest kind of biological drama. Predator and prey. I wouldn't have to suffer the anger of knowing that pollutants in our environment killed me or the agony of knowing that misogyny kept the health industry from adequately funding research into the prevention of breast cancer. There would be no blame in a death at the paws and teeth of a mountain lion. Just pure biology.

As I lay there with my eyes closed, knowing that I wouldn't hear the paw pads on the stone, I did try to conjure the fear I knew I should feel. But fear is a little like a star: the more directly you look at it, the more it fades. I wondered if fear weren't really just very concentrated loneliness—I am alone, I might be disappeared altogether, I am prey.

By accepting myself as an animal in a web of living beings on Earth, might the loneliness ease? Maybe I had it right as a child after all, scouting out potential homes in nearby woods and under freeway overpasses, looking for blackberry brambles and other food sources. Loneliness is fearing our bodies won't be cared for—fed, sheltered, held. But we are all feral, no matter how hard we pretend otherwise with our laws, our architecture, our attempts to control even DNA. Perhaps those people who wanted to shoot the cats in the Patterson's trailer were only acting on their own feral natures, an urge so deep and, in their cases, unchecked, that they followed it as surely as a mountain lion would follow a deer scent.

The fear of mountain lions is biological, hardwired into us. It's the fear of predation. The fear of being prey. Humans have no other real competitors for habitat, nor any other large predator. The closest is the grizzly bear, which coexists with humans only in Alaska. Cougars are the last top-of-the-food-chain carnivore that still reside in the lower forty-eight states in any numbers.

The truth is, the mountain lion has outwitted us just a bit. We haven't hunted them out of existence. We haven't even been able to study them very successfully. They evade us on all counts. Mountain lions give us the feeling of being out of control and that's a feeling most people don't like. The mountain lion, as a predator and competitor for habitat, reminds us that we are animals, nothing more and nothing less. These carnivores call into question what it means to be human, and that, apparently, is terrifying.

For centuries, philosophers and scientists have tried to prove that people are separate from, a cut above, other animals. They have argued that we are closer to god. The only creatures able to reason. To use tools. To feel. To make art. The rationalizations for our assumed superiority are many and change over the centuries and decades as each one is disproved. Every year we learn different ways in which other animals use tools, like the chimpanzees who use grass stalks to harvest termites from holes. I have witnessed mother harbor seals using their flippers as ramps for their young to wiggle out of the water and up onto the beach. Some female dolphins harvest ocean sponges, which they carry when foraging for food, perhaps to scoop prey out of hiding places on the sea floor. Scientists also have evidence that bears know how to medicate themselves with specific kinds of plants. You don't have to be a scientist to know that animals feel deeply; this can be learned by simply living with a cat or dog. A perhaps trickier issue is whether animals have the ability to make art, but I'm convinced that the songs of humpback whales, passed from whale to whale across the oceans, is art. The ability to reason? Humans plunder and pollute. We destroy our own. Who is to say what is reasonable?

It is said that the human biological advantage is our big brain, but even that is seriously limited. In fact, some of the most interesting research in animal cognition involves the much bigger brains of whales and the attempt to understand what they could be using all those brain cells for. The answer, some researchers speculate, lies in the *whaleness* of those big brains, in the fact that *we* are the ones without enough understanding, from our limited human point of view, to see the vast knowledge or function of all those whale brain cells. Nature rarely creates waste. Those brain cells are doing *something*. We just don't know what.

And that's what *I* want to know. I want to know what *they*—the whales, mountain lions, even tarantulas—know. I want in on the secrets of other species.

This isn't about reason. Measuring the dollar value of a mountain lion hunting tag or livestock losses is far easier than measuring the value of a cougar's beauty, independence, and grace. We don't know how to calculate the value of the mountain lion, and perhaps that in itself is its value.

There are, in fact, good scientific reasons for protecting mountain lions. As Steve Bobzien puts it, "Super carnivores are barometers of the habitat." Because carnivores are high in the food chain, they play an integral role in moving energy through the ecosystem, a critical process on which all living things depend. As Kevin Hansen writes, "Whether humans believe it or not, we're players in the same game." And the game cannot be played without all the players.

But maybe we don't need scientific reasons for accepting the mountain lion as a member of our community. Perhaps the greatest value of the mountain lion is that it can teach us humility. Perhaps by accepting that we are animals striving for survival and comfort like all other animals, we can begin to find a harmony that is so often missing in our communities.

That evening I spent at Lake Chabot was a beautiful one. After getting up from my stone bed, I walked farther along the east shore trail, where mountain lions had been sighted, than I had planned. Away from the bigger cities, dusk is weightier, seems to almost have density. Stark silver snags struck graceful poses over the flat, green water, while geese flew overhead in formation. A light breeze kept the cloud of gnats at bay. Having learned that it was tarantula mating season, I searched the path for more gargantuan spiders but didn't see any.

Nor did I see any deer carcasses or mountain lions.

It was pitch dark by the time I got back to the Lake Chabot parking lot. I did feel a little nervous by then, a little out of control. I did look over my shoulder a lot. But I *liked* that feeling of knowing that I was just one more animal scurrying home for safety.

In fact, I like being a member of a biologically diverse community so much that I recently moved to a neighborhood adjacent to Tilden Regional Park in Berkeley. A couple of weeks ago, I walked on a wooded trail only a few hundred yards from my home, looking for hints of spring. I came upon what had recently been a huge puddle. The stretch of trail had dried into a smooth bed of damp mud. Striding gloriously across that bed of damp mud was a set of enormous tracks. They were about four inches in diameter. The main pad looked like two merged hearts, and the four toe pads were tear-shaped. The main difference between dog and cat tracks is the presence of claw marks. Cats walk with their claws retracted. Dogs cannot retract their claws. Though other tracks in this perfectly smooth bed of mud showed distinct toenails, these biggest tracks didn't have a trace of claw marks. They could not have been anything but mountain lion tracks, and they were fresh. Perhaps the big cat was nearby, even watching me. I stood very still in this habitat I shared with the mountain lion and learned an even deeper meaning of prey.

Dead Horse Pass

Katie and I hiked out of the town of Ten Sleep into Wyoming's Bighorn Mountains in the pouring rain. We had ten days—ten sleeps, in fact—of hiking ahead of us, with only one planned layover day, near the end of the trip, on which we hoped to climb Cloud Peak. Committed to the goal of reaching that summit, we killed ourselves hiking long days on hard trails to preserve the layover day. We reached the base camp for the climb late one evening, pumped water from the lake in the dark, and fell into the sack.

By five the next morning we were firing up the stove. After tea and hot cereal, we set off, primed in the glorious dawn, for Cloud Peak. To our surprise, we found another camper at the far end of our lake, a lone fisherman who already had a roaring fire going in his camp which was littered with fishing gear. I inquired about the fishing and he assured us that he had done very well with his pole and line. Though he didn't ask us what we were doing, Katie offered that we were off to climb Cloud Peak. He doubted, out loud, that we would be able to accomplish that. The mountain was, after all, over thirteen thousand feet high. As we hiked away from his camp, an uncomfortable feeling crawled up my back. It had something to do with how I felt that now we *had* to climb Cloud Peak. Our day of play had become something more; we had something to prove.

Nothing beckons a will-driven personality more relentlessly than a summit. Nothing screams the word "goal" more loudly. Why, I've asked myself many times, does standing on a summit mean so much? Is the pursuit of the top of a mountain an empty goal? Is it a sign of spiritual weakness to long for summits? A sign that the will has become besot with too much power?

When I was twenty, when my feet still felt like wings, when joy itself fueled my climbs, I could easily answer that nagging question about the meaning of summits. I remember climbing Mount Rainer—called Tahoma, meaning simply "the mountain," by the Yakima Indians—and how my mind and heart united in heaving upward, stepping, moving to the demands of the mountain, as if it, the mountain, were the only god I needed. One foot followed the other, knowing to step over this small crevasse, to go around another. And I believed in the mountain wholly, its life-giving capacity, the way its icy peak collected clouds, squeezed the rain out of them, fed rivers, replenished trout-filled lakes, nurtured forests of deer, roots, berries, and marmots for hundreds of miles around. Without the summit, none of this, no *life*, would be possible.

Summits are less easily won for me now, and so making peace with them is also more difficult. Even so, I still know the solace they bring, how pitting myself against rock alone relieves my mind and heart and soul like nothing else. It is definitely more than proving something. And yet, once that fisherman put the challenge to us, proof became inextricably part of the equation. And when it did, a disorientation set in.

A few miles out from the base camp, I became confused about our location. I'm a good map reader and wilderness navigator, but this terrain was a mess of peaks, several of which were similar in elevation, none of which seemed to have distinctive landforms. We studied the map and compass for an uncomfortably long time, finally determining our coordinates and choosing a route up the peak. Yet even after we climbed the tall mountain of sharp, bear-sized boulders and stood on the summit, I felt disoriented.

Even so, it was a good day, and we descended the mountain happy in our doses of endorphins. Near the bottom of the mountain, we sat on a hot rock to rest. I pulled out the maps again and this time, finally, we realized where we were. We had not climbed Cloud Peak. Instead we had climbed a peak that was two hundred feet lower in elevation and a short distance west of Cloud Peak.

We did have a sense of humor about our mistake. And we carried on a lofty discussion about the illusory quality of goals, how we had missed our intended summit by a couple of hundred feet in altitude and a half mile in horizontal geography, but hey, we climbed a mountain and had a great day. The summit poses as a goal but is really just the means to a day of climbing.

Having reached the trail at last, bounding back to camp at dusk, looking forward to a pot of couscous, we approached the fisherman's camp.

I asked Katie, "Are we going to tell him we didn't climb Cloud Peak?"

"We're not going to lie."

I fell silent, guilty that I had considered lying. After all, I had climbed many peaks as high as and higher than Cloud Peak, and wasn't that, in this case anyway, really the issue? Whether or not two girls could climb any mountain? I said as much to Katie, but she insisted that she wasn't going to lie.

Okay, she was right, there was more dignity in the truth, in not taking on his warped frame of mind. Why should I let myself get sucked into his view of climbing and women? We knew what we had accomplished and were able to accomplish. And anyway, it was the journey that mattered. He had become a part of our journey, a summit of integrity.

There he was, flipping a pan of trout at his campfire. We tromped along toward his camp, Katie in the lead. I could tell by her pace and the way she held her head that she had decided to say nothing at all if she could help it.

"Howdy, girls."

"Hello," we answered in unison.

"Did you reach the top of the mountain?"

"Sure did," Katie sang out. "It was a great day."

Stunned, I followed her down the trail until we were out of earshot. "You said you were going to tell him the truth."

"I did. He asked if we had reached the top of the mountain. He didn't specify *which* mountain."

Summits are like coyotes. Tricksters. They often appear where they didn't seem to exist. They recede during a climb. Or become an entirely different mountain. The summit of Cloud Peak may have been offering a lesson, or at least posing a question. If you get the joy, but not the summit, have you accomplished your climbing goal?

An alternative health care provider who was treating me for a cycling injury once accused me of adventuring only because I was addicted to endorphins. As if my bike rides, mountain climbs, and backcountry skis were unhealthy, junkie behaviors. As if I were uselessly trashing my body. She suggested that the highs I tried to tell her about were fleeting, temporary. Compared, I supposed, to a *real* spiritual practice. She did hand me some passages from a text by some guru.

I wanted to hand her back some passages from John Muir. I had always suspected that his body produced endorphins, that natural narcotic, in unnaturally high amounts. The man was spiritually feral. Just reading him can be hallucinatory. His daring wasn't a kind of courage so much as a wild relationship to joy. I love how so many of his adventures began with his putting on a heavy overcoat and stuffing the pockets with crusts of bread. He would stride from camp, having no idea if he was off for a couple of hours or a couple of days. His joy in the wilderness was so intense it *did* sound as if he were tripping. In the essay "Snow-Storms" he wrote about wanting to experience an avalanche, not visually but kinetically. So one day, near the summit of a climb, he entered a canyon into which a lot of snow had been funneled. Suddenly, he was "swished down to the foot of the canyon as if by enchantment." While most mountaineers put a great deal of effort into *avoiding* avalanches, Muir wrote of his descent: "This flight in what might be called a milky way of snow-stars was the most spiritual and exhilarating of all the modes of motion I have ever experienced. Elijah's flight in a chariot of fire could hardly have been more gloriously exciting."

I believe that John Muir was not exaggerating. I believe him literally. For Muir, the beauty of what he encountered in the wilderness, the high, was always more important than the moments of overcoming obstacles. Or reaching summits.

Yet, Muir kept climbing. And I keep climbing. And the truth is, no one gets to the top of a mountain without a healthy dose of will. Is that the darker side of summits?

Dead Horse Pass wasn't even a true summit, just a pass into the next valley, but a crucial one on this two-week hike in the Rockies. This time Katie and I were in the High Uintas, the only range in the Rockies that runs east and west rather than north and south. We had wanted to hike the entire range, so we'd placed a classified ad in a Salt Lake City newspaper offering a hundred dollars for a ride to the trailhead. Janice, a woman who lived on a ranch in Wyoming, answered the ad and drove us from our car at one end of the trail to the other end. She kindly insisted that we hike out and call her if we ran into trouble. She would fetch us and return us to our vehicle at any time.

We saw only two other parties the entire two weeks we were in the Uintas, a range of high broad meadows and long blue skies. We hiked happily, counting the miles, making sure we would get out in the allotted days to our car at trail's end.

Dead Horse Pass was the last climb of the trip, and when we reached it we were surprised to find that it was very steep and buried in snow. At the bottom of the slope—really a cliff—were angular boulders and a hard cold lake. We needed a rope, ice axes, and crampons. I knew it was a risk we shouldn't take. After all, we had Janice's phone number and her willingness to pick us up and drive us to our car. We had wanted, though, to hike the entire range, from east to west. On the other side of Dead Horse Pass there were only two days of hiking to complete this goal. My will seemed to actually roar in my ears.

Fear is supposed to run interference for the will. It is supposed to say, I know you want this, but don't you see, it isn't good for you. You will lose. You may die.

That the lure of summits often out-shouts this voice says a lot about the potency of summits. About how badly some of us want them.

After some discussion about our route, we decided on straight up, to get it over with as quickly as possible, rather than traversing the slope, making our own switchbacks and giving ourselves more chances to slip and fall. I took the lead, kicking a deep stairway into the nearly vertical slope of snow. One slip and we'd slide a very long way to the bottom of this pass, the speed of our slide creating a momentum that would meet the sharp boulders below. I concentrated every ounce of my will into kicking steps that would hold both me and Katie. My immediate goal was a patch of exposed rock halfway up the slope, but when I reached that I found that it was even less stable than the snow. Shards of talus lay on top of a sliding mud. There was nothing to dig steps into, just moving earth, and the only thing that kept me going was a mental momentum, a will to move upward and forward, even as the steep talus and mud slope worked like gravity's devil to suck me back down the pass.

Surely that boulder a few feet above me was stable. I reached it, grabbed on, and it too slid as easily as a bowling ball on a slick lane—down toward Katie. I shouted. The boulder missed her. The next few minutes held only my heaving breath, as somehow we defied gravity and made it up the mountain.

At the top, I dropped to my knees, stunned. I picked up a small, flat, rectangular piece of blue-green talus. A bit of the summit. What I had risked my life to reach. The edgy rock sat in my hand, innocent of its allure, and I realized how tiny it was, this summit piece, this goal.

And yet, already in those first summit moments, a new knowledge colonized my cells. Not just an endorphin high but a knowledge that I knew would last. If this were just a hormonal squirt to the brain it would be illusory. It would fade. Likewise, if this were just my will being a despot, another accomplishment to tick off, the satisfaction of reaching the summit would evaporate with my sweat. But the feeling I had then, the intensity of those rocks beneath my knees and hands—as well as the very idea of standing on the continental divide—was folded into my being permanently.

I had been right when I was twenty, when my feet still felt like wings, when joy itself fueled my body. My bit of talus was just a little rock but it supported the entire mountain below it. Summits do serve a godly function by collecting clouds, wringing out precipitation, providing the slope for streams to run down and the valleys for lakes to collect in, and ultimately nourishing all plants and animals. In this way, summits have the same kind of ecological importance as mountain lions, serving as the apexes of the flow of resources. Being here was a way to pay homage.

Yet, this time, I became intensely aware of another presence beneath me. That piece of talus in my hand held much, much more than the earthy bulk of the mountain. It also held all the *space* below me, the freefall. It held everything I *didn't* know, and ignorance is the biggest wilderness of all. Which is why, even though I didn't actually fall off that mountain, I'm still reeling.

Perhaps it isn't will at all that fuels a person to the top of a mountain. Perhaps it is an ache for beauty. A desire to be dangled over the canyon of nothingness. To, in fact, *lose* one's will for a moment. Perhaps climbing a mountain is nothing more than an act of worship, and reaching the barren perch of a summit is to experience pure awe.

I stayed on the top of Dead Horse Pass for as long as I could endure the great unknowingness. Then, as a light snow began to fall, we descended into the valley on the other side.

Girl with Boat

In spite of my insistence on being a land person, someone who has stuck to the deserts and mountains, the forests and glaciers, the sea has persistently toyed with my unconscious. Sea mammals appear regularly in my dreams.

For example, I'm hiking in the desert, stepping around the woody remains of Joshua trees, avoiding the dagger-thorns of cacti, trying to endure the sight of endless pale sand. I come upon a dolphin lying in the sand, emaciated, its eyes scratchy-red, a tiny lift and fall of its mid-body suggesting the last breath of life.

Another time I'm hiking down a terraced garden, long-abandoned and overgrown, pushing through the shrubbery, the tangle of green. I come upon an old-fashioned swimming pool, cracked and made of gray cement. Most of the cavity is taken up by the body of a big gray whale, wiggling as best it can in the bit of water surrounding its massive body.

Still another time, I'm escaping something, I don't know what, at night in an urban landscape. The stench of factory waste and burning fuel permeates the air I breathe. I run until I reach the edge of land and consider making my way through a maze of sinister-seeming wharves and docks. I stop, though, because these are covered with sea lions, dark brown, stinky sea lions snorting and watching me as I enter the water, there being nowhere else for me to go.

Clearly, all of these dreamworld sea mammals are in trouble. Their desperation frightens me. But fear is a giant arrow, a flashing neon sign, a crooked finger beckoning. Maybe it was time to look in the direction of the arrow, heed the sign, walk toward the finger. Approach, in other words, the sea.

The words lagoon, sound, slough, estuary, tidal pool, delta, and even shore, are more seductive than scary. They describe the liminal bodies of water. The edges. The transitions. The places where sea meets continent and also where land animals meet sea creatures.

The Salmon River in Oregon is not wide, long, or deep. It's just an ordinary blue-green river meandering through farmland and forests. Just before reaching the sea, the Salmon River turns sharply west, and over the centuries it has been laying down deposits of sand at its estuary, creating a long spit of beach, curling into the ocean.

I went to spend a week in a house on the inland riverbank where I could look across the river to this spit of beach and beyond to the ocean. I intended to spend the week writing, reading, and venturing out daily to hike in the coastal mountains and canoe across the river to the beach for high- and low-tide walks.

On the first morning of my stay, I awoke to find the estuary busy with wildlife. A great blue heron spent the early hours ostensibly hunting but mostly just posing on seaweed-covered river stones, imitating bird images in Japanese paintings. Grebes, golden eyes, and cormorants made appearances, as did a bald eagle, circling high overhead scanning for opportunity. With binoculars plastered to my eyes, I spent the morning monitoring everyone's fishing successes, intending on getting to work soon.

But the late morning high tide brought to my private outdoor theater an even more dramatic wildlife show. Several fat seals came in with the tide to spend the afternoon lounging on the sand just across the river, not a hundred yards from my riverbank perch. I knew that the seals' rookery was located around the big headland to the north. Often they swam and played in the river, but I'd never seen so many—I counted twelve now—sunning on the spit. With the especially fat adult seals were three oversized slugs that I realized were newborn pups. This bit of beach, then, was the seal nursery. In the relative calm of the estuary, the pups learned their first lessons in how to survive at sea.

Right away I noticed differences in the seals' personalities and appearances, and I named them accordingly. There was Gnarly Mom, one of the ugliest seals I'd ever seen. Her face looked like a prizefighter's, flat and misshapen, and her hide was covered with scars and irregular coloring. Her pup was a tiny replica of her, so I named it Gnarly Pup. They lay side by side on the beach, with Gnarly Pup nursing from time to time, almost visibly growing fat on the rich seal milk. Then there was the perfect mother who spent the entire afternoon teaching her pup skills, wasting no time lounging on the beach. I named her Soccer Mom and her gorgeous progeny Spotted Pup. They were constantly in and out of the water, swimming laps in the estuary, working on diving and fishing skills. A few teenagers spent the high-tide hours in the warm sun with the moms and pups, and an occasional adult male would also haul out on the beach for a while.

The least interesting seal I simply called "the white one." She appeared dead, though through my binoculars I caught an occasional flick of whiskers as she lay on the beach hour after hour without moving. She was unquestionably the fattest seal and her white coat made her stand out even more.

A couple of mornings into my stay on the Salmon River estuary, I got up early, determined to work rather than waste another entire day staring at the shorebirds and seals. Besides, a storm was coming in. The clouds gathered, darkened, and lowered. The wind picked up until there were wavelets on the estuary. I wondered if the seals would come to the spit for the day even though there would be no sun for basking, but they swam in as usual with the incoming tide and huddled together on the beach. I supposed the young ones would be safer here than at sea in a storm. The fat white seal lolled on the beach and looked as if she were groaning.

I turned my back on the wind whipping across the river, the seals, and the crashing waves just beyond. I went to work at my computer.

At high tide, when the storm was peaking, I stepped over to the window to check the seals. Peering through the rainy sky, I saw to my astonishment a new, thin, wormlike creature lying on the sand next to the fat white seal whose body had a big indent, like a saddle, in the middle. She had given birth.

White Mom lay as if she were dead, as if giving birth had expended every bit of her energy. She wasn't nursing her newborn as I had watched the other mothers do all week. How long could a newborn last without nursing? Surely not very long. And yet White Mom showed no interest in her pup, whom I named High Tide.

My anxiety grew as the tide slackened and then began draining back out to sea. Still, White Mom paid no attention to her pup. Meanwhile, Soccer Mom was teaching Spotted Pup how to fish in stormy weather. They dove, swam fast laps, hauled out onto the spit, and then slid back into the river. Surely Soccer Mom would alert the others to the child neglect taking place just a few yards down the beach.

By now the river, helped by the storm and falling tide, was whooshing out to sea. High Tide was recovering from the birth experience and had begun to wiggle. I hoped that she knew instinctively about nursing and that she would inch over to her mother's belly for a meal. Instead, she squirmed to the edge of the spit. From there she flopped herself into the river.

Seals are born knowing how to swim. Even so, each time one of the pups went into the water its mom followed, keeping close tabs. Not so White Mom. She didn't budge. High Tide had been born only an hour or so earlier. The tide and river current were moving very fast and there was still a good storm blowing. The big exhausted seal didn't seem to have even noticed that her pup had dived into the river.

Meanwhile, High Tide was being washed to sea. All by herself. With my binoculars trained on her tiny, slick gray head, I watched as the newborn bobbed seaward. She tried, two or three times, to reverse the direction of her movement, back toward her mother. I saw her turn her nose upstream and *try*. But it was no use. Her pup strength couldn't match the tidal current. In a matter of moments, she was gone.

I was bereft. By now I was standing outside in the rain, on the riverbank, shouting at White Mom to get off the beach and go get her baby. I seriously considered getting in my canoe and paddling out to try to rescue the seal pup myself. Or to prod White Mom off the beach. Either action would have put me in violation of the Marine Mammal Protection Act, but of course that wasn't the point. Seals work out their births on a yearly basis without my help.

Still, I felt desperate. And even angry. White Mom's negligence was ruining my retreat week. I didn't want to witness the abandonment and probable death of a seal pup. I tried to remind myself how nature can be cruel. Birth is a risky process. Newborns of all species die. All the time. And a baby having the misfortune of being born at high tide in a bad storm would have even less of a chance at survival than one born in fairer conditions.

Forty-five minutes after High Tide was swept to sea, White Mom lifted her head and moseyed, as if she were barely alive, to the edge of the spit and slunk in. The current carried her to sea as well. It was far too late for her to find her pup, who was surely floundering alone in the Pacific, if not already drowned.

I couldn't remove myself from my perch overlooking the river. I waited. I scanned the blurry, rain-soaked estuary with my binoculars. I could hardly bear it. It was as if I had gotten stuck inside one of my sea mammal dreams.

A couple of hours after White Mom went off, presumably in search of her pup, I was amazed to see High Tide herself come struggling back up the river. The tidal current was weaker now, and by staying close to the spit, she swam upstream in the eddies. Though White Mom was nowhere in sight, and I knew High Tide couldn't survive without her, I had a bit of hope.

Until I witnessed the newborn trying to overcome the next obstacle. Seals need land for resting and breathing. The only land High Tide had known was that bit of spit, and somehow she knew she should return there. By now, however, not only were the rest of the seals gone but the outgoing tide had ripped away the edge of the spit. To get up on the beach, the pup would have to climb a one-foot-high sand cliff. During the week, I had seen the cows use their flippers as ramps, placing them against the small cliff so that their pups could slide up onto the beach. High Tide's mom was not around to provide this service, and I watched the newborn trying, time and again, struggling with her just-hours-old flippers to gain a purchase and get up on the beach.

She became exhausted and drifted seaward. The ride on the tide gave her a moment to rest and she managed to swim upstream again. This happened several times, where she tried to climb out on the bank, lost all her strength, washed seaward, turned around, and tried again. Finally she gave up and was flushed out to sea, disappearing from sight altogether.

An hour later White Mom returned, somewhat more energetic, looking for her pup. I wondered if seals feel grief. Why wouldn't they? White Mom climbed out on the beach and waited for High Tide, even as it grew dark.

The next morning I resolved to cut my ties to the estuary wildlife and get some work done, which I did until midday when I made a sandwich and ventured to the window. The tide was coming in again and soon Soccer Mom and Spotted Pup frolicked up the river and climbed onto the beach. Gnarly Mom and Gnarly Pup arrived as well, as did a couple of adolescents.

I turned my back for a few minutes to make a cup of tea and when I returned there was White Mom. And at her side, nursing, was High Tide!

Although White Mom remained a lazy mother, much preferring lounging on the beach to teaching her pup how to fish, she did nurse High Tide the rest of that week, and I was able to leave my estuary satisfied that they both would survive, on land and at sea.

And yet a sadness lingered. I felt left out. I had remained on the terrestrial sidelines, trying to work, typing words into a computer, while Gnarly Mom and Gnarly Pup, Soccer Mom and Spotted Pup, White Mom and High Tide partook of the primordial soup. What had they been doing that week beyond what I could observe? That feeling I'd had while searching for mountain lions, of wanting to know the cougarness of cougars, returned. I still wanted in on the secrets of other species. The allure of my ongoing sea mammal dreams—in which orcas, humpbacks, porpoises, harbor and elephant seals splashed through my unconscious—intensified.

But how does a human being come to understand seals? My approach so far had been entirely unscientific. I had shamelessly anthropomorphized the seals at the Salmon River estuary. And yet, the more I read the work of wildlife biologists, the more I thought the whole notion of anthropomorphizing had been demonized a bit too much. After all, we *are* humans. How can we *not* look at the world through our human lens? In fact, I'd argue that it's anthropo-centric to believe our viewpoint can ever be objective, that we have the godlike ability to choose and use an omniscient point of view. Assuming we are capable of objectivity is a denial of the rich ecological context in which we live. We can *only* view other animals from our own species' eyes. Wouldn't it be better to just accept that than to pretend we can put it aside? I have even wondered if some wildlife biologists insist on objective observation simply because it's too hard to deal with emotional involvement.

In my experience, human empathy and compassion are excellent tools for learning about other species. Luckily, this point of view has the support of some (though far from all) wildlife experts. I once heard Jane Goodall explain that Louis Leakey had hired her to study the chimpanzees not because of her scientific background (she had practically none) but because of her tremendous love for animals. She told how, soon after moving in with the chimps, she began noting their individual personalities as well as their expressions of emotion toward each other and toward her. She named all of the chimps she came to know. Other scientists wasted no time in dis-counting her work. Not only was naming one's subjects considered highly unscientific, but attributing emotions to these beasts, well, that was absurd. Next, she'd be saying they were nearly human.

As Goodall has pointed out, any child who has had a dog or cat knows that animals have a range of emotional responses. And any child who has had more than one dog or cat knows that other animals have differing personalities, just as people do. Of course, eventually, Goodall even proved that chimps use tools, rocking the worlds of those people who needed to regard tool-making as the sole province of humans. When Goodall reported her discovery to Leakey, he made his famous remark: "Now we must redefine tool, redefine Man, or accept chimpanzees as humans." We have, since then, been frantically trying to redefine ourselves.

Roger Payne, famed for studying the songs of humpback whales, wrote in his book *Among Whales,* "There seems to be an inborn refusal in many humans to accept the possibility that the mental abilities of our species might be in any way unremarkable in comparison to others." Payne has spent most of his life studying whales and believes that they must be doing something phenomenal with their very large brains, something important enough to justify the huge metabolic expense of maintaining such structures. He suggests—although he is careful to point out that there is no hard data to back the idea—that the complicated brains of whales *could* indicate that they're smarter than us.

Like Goodall, Payne is a wildlife scientist who loves his subjects and this love breeds a deep respect. I believe that the willingness of these researchers to use the full range of human response—including intuition, reason, love, and fear—brings them closer to truly understanding their subjects than those wildlife scientists who use an approach that believes itself to be objective.

No one has respected sea mammals more nor understood them better—for they depended upon them for their livelihood—than the Inuit people who live throughout the Arctic regions. Happily for me, Inuit knowledge of sea mammals led to an invention that allows me to get closer to the creatures.

The Inuits invented sea kayaks somewhere between two to eight thousand years ago. These elegant and ingenious boats were constructed from wood, bone, and seal and caribou skin. The design of the modern sea kayak has changed very little from the original Inuit design; only the materials have changed. The Inuits also made waterproof, breathable jackets out of the intestines of fish and seals. They purposely left openings in the seams of these jackets and then stuffed these openings with feathers. The openings allowed for a flow of air in and out of the jacket, while the feathers shed seawater, keeping the paddler dry.

If I was going to take the next step in getting to know sea mammals, following in the paddle strokes of the Inuit people seemed like the best move. But that meant getting *in* the sea rather than bobbing in a big vessel on top of it or standing at the edge of it. How scary could that be? Everyone knows that we all came from the sea in the first place. We're still coming from the sea, in a sense. The amniotic fluid of mammals is amazingly similar to seawater, containing the same salts in almost the exact same proportions. Each mammal birth can be viewed as a reenactment of this prehistoric emergence from the sea to land. The sea is the nursery of all life. Where life was first created. The place of creativity.

It was time to go back.

And yet kayaks scared me. The first time I tried kayaking, twenty-five years ago, had been a miserable failure. I was working as a ranger at Mount Rainier National Park and my high school friend Ross invited me to a party on an island in Puget Sound. He and his other friend were the only men present that weekend. The rest of the guests were women—to my young eyes, very tough women. I remember watching them hoist themselves onto a rope swing, fly out over the sound, and splash from a great height into the salty water. Compared to their vitality, Ross's taciturn friend seemed oddly safe. I can still picture him, skinny and bare chested, scraggly hair, standing waist deep in the sound, his hand gently rocking a kayak. He suggested that he teach me how to roll the boat.

I should have known the second I wedged myself into the small, boy-sized cockpit that this was a bad idea, but by then he was already securing the spray skirt around me. His only instructions were, "Twist your body."

Then he capsized the kayak. I hung upside down in the ice-cold seawater, feeling as if I were permanently locked into the boat above me. I panicked and thrashed.

Eventually, he wrenched one of my shoulders and my head up above the surface of the water. I sucked in air as he gave more detailed instructions: "Twist your hips." He dropped my heavy head into the water and again I hung upside down.

I don't remember what happened after that. I may have succeeded in rolling the kayak. Probably not. I may have managed to pop out of the spray skirt and cockpit. Or perhaps my "teacher" rescued me. I do remember noticing the feral girls still whooping and splashing from their rope swing as I scuttled up to the shore.

So I let a couple of decades go by, sea mammals still haunting my dreams, but too chicken to enter *their* world. In fact, I might have said something to the effect of, "You couldn't pay me to get back in one of those skinny boats." Until somebody did pay me to get in a kayak.

A local newspaper, for which I'd done a lot of outdoors writing, hired me to do a story on urban kayaking. Perhaps I believed the human construct of a big city would protect me from the wildness of the sea. My first class, me alone with two instructors, was in the Oakland harbor, surrounded by the upscale buildings of urban renewal as well as the bombed-out buildings of a past industrial era. A snowy egret stood on one yellow foot and watched, not three yards away from where I climbed into the cockpit of a kayak for the second time in my life. The gorgeous bird whose feathers were indeed snowy, with delicate tufts hanging off its chest, had long black pencil legs and a yellow and black beak to match its feet and legs.

"Who're you looking at?" I asked the bird, unable to be impressed with its beauty right then. I could think only of hanging upside down in icy saltwater, trapped in a kayak.

And yet the second I pushed off from the shore I knew I had found a new and profound way back to the wild. The buoyancy of the water upon which I sat rose right up through my body to my head. This was the opposite of the gravity-defying act of climbing a mountain; the sea held me, rocked me, allowed me to slip through it. A kayak is a partner with the sea. It isn't ridden or captained like other boats. It's not a third party negotiating between you and the sea. A sea kayak is worn, becomes a part of your body. I had acquired a sea creature bottom half.

Soon I was kayaking everywhere in the San Francisco Bay and its contributing rivers and deltas and eventually out the Golden Gate. But the first time I ventured into the open sea, I paddled out from Half Moon Bay. That day, the sky was steel gray and the air crackled with electricity. Ten foot swells announced the coming storm. When I was in the trough of one of these swells, I couldn't see my kayaking companions at all. I was surrounded by sloped walls of water. My virgin skills, paired up with the high seas, produced a strange joy. I hadn't grown up kayaking as I had grown up cycling and climbing, and the innocence gave me fresh humility. I was at the mercy of the sea, an environment over which I had no control. The simplicity of this match—a girl in a boat and the sea—freed me. There was nothing for me to do but ride the swells and let the motion of the ocean rock a new kind of grace into my body.

Eventually, my kayak and I made our way to Alaska, where the surrounding waters are rich feeding grounds for seals, sea lions, and all kinds of whales. I had been to Alaska many times before to hike the mountains and view the northern lights. There is nothing I like better than to lie on my back on a cold, dark Alaskan night and look up at a sky pulsing and swirling with green and red and purple. Even more amazing than the intensity of color is the physical pull I feel from the movement of light, as if the motion moves the blood through my veins. The Inuit people say that northern lights are torches carried by spirits to guide nomadic travelers. Cosmic mentors. I have long thought that I qualified for their services.

This time, however, I was going to Alaska to be rocked by its sea rather than the solar storms in its skies. My friends and I started in Glacier Bay National Park, kayaking out from the park headquarters into a thick mist and light drizzle. We entered an archipelago of small islands and little bays and by afternoon had somehow become lost. The rising tide had drowned some tiny landmark islands and altered the shape of the shorelines of bigger islands. The low-lying fog, too, made any long distance navigation impossible. I knew we weren't *very* lost, that we'd soon get oriented, and so I just paddled and let the others find our way, which they soon did. In the late afternoon, we reentered the big body of water we knew to be the homeward bay. As we sat in our kayaks, reluctant to return to camp, I was lulled by the lapping water sounds and swirling mist. Soon our six kayaks drifted apart, so that we could hardly see one another, as we listened to a splashing in the distance that we guessed to be the tail of a humpback whale.

I was alone by the time I saw the whale's spout. Alone in the sense that I could no longer see my human companions. But there were more whales. One spouted behind me and another to my left. And then another and another. I slowly came to realize that the bay was full of whales, their slick dark backs arcing out of the still water, their spouts shooting up through the drizzling mist.

I sat very still, listening and watching, until a mounded whale back broke the surface of the water twenty yards from my kayak. I might have tried to get out of the way if I'd known which direction to paddle or if I'd thought I could paddle fast enough. But I didn't. I held my paddle across the deck of my boat, gripping it with both hands. The mounded whale back rolled forward and the fluke flapped briefly in the air before the whale dove directly under my kayak.

I wasn't afraid. If its back bumped the bottom of my boat and flipped me, and if I actually made contact with the beast, I would no doubt slide right off its body, maybe cutting myself on some barnacles that gripped its hide. But that didn't happen. The surface of the water was hardly disturbed as the whale slid below me. I could see the dark form moving slowly, and I imagined the humpback rolling its giant eyeballs upward, checking out this fake mermaid. I like to think that the whale knew exactly what I was, because in that moment *I* knew exactly what I was. Ah, the whale and I might have thought in unison, girl with boat.

The Black Wolf

The water of Adams Inlet, on the eastern side of Glacier Bay, buoyed me and my kayak. Rain had fallen for ten days and would fall for the next ten days. This morning it had joined forces with the wind, driving into the faces of me and my companions as we paddled north from the mouth of Muir Inlet. My kayak galloped over the waves, rising on the crests, slamming down into the troughs. But now at dusk, floating on the perfectly flat and still water in this cove, it was only misting. Pockets of fog moved like genies across the surface of the water, obscuring a portion of the shoreline momentarily, then revealing the short beach of driftwood backed by a steeply climbing bank of evergreens. The green in Alaska is the deepest possible, and the silence that evening was as deep as the green.

Until the one note was sung, a long hollow sound. Soon it was answered, or perhaps joined, by another voice. The word howl, so often applied to wolves, is all wrong. Howl sounds too sheer, too desperate, too anguished. The wind this morning howled, but these wolves in Adams Inlet lowed a mellow music, more trombone than trumpet, relaxed and satisfied.

The ocean cradled me in my kayak. The green-black trees soothed my eyes. The wolf voices wove like silk threads through the mist. I wanted to stay much longer, but the angled light permeating the fog was dusky, and dusk in an Alaskan August comes very late. I turned my back on the wolf symphony regretfully, and we paddled back out of Adams Inlet to make camp at the mouth.

That night, while we were firing up the stoves and throwing together the tents, Georgena, a woman I had met only at the beginning of this trip, stopped what she was doing and smiled at me. "You look so comfortable out here," she said. "You look like this is where you belong."

Her observation made me happy. I was coming home again and I liked that it showed. I kept the comment close to my heart through several more days of paddling. We finally reached our northernmost destination, McBride Glacier, and set up camp at the mouth of the cove. Every few minutes an explosion sounded as another chunk of the glacier calved into the sea.

After dinner I hiked alone toward the foot of the tidewater glacier, climbing first on the hillside and then dropping down to a sandy beach. There I found a set of very fresh—the tide had just withdrawn—wolf tracks. I followed the tracks until I reached a good place to sit on a rock and watch the glacier calve into the bay. I never saw the wolf.

That night, though, as we crawled into our tents, we heard a pack of them conversing. The baying seemed to come from just up the hill, not far at all, and sounded less like music and more like warning. This time we weren't floating in our boats on the water, we were camped on their beach. Still, I wasn't fearful. Not very, anyway. I crawled into my tent and fell easily asleep.

Wolves sound just like dogs. They *are* dogs, of course. But somehow it's surprising when they behave just like them. I awoke to hear snuffling. Someone was circumnavigating my tent, checking out all the smells. I searched my memory for the times I had cheated and brought food into my tent, as if by locating the memory I could somehow erase the act. The snuffling continued. I spoke softly, saying, "Git. Git away from here." I tried to go back to sleep, desperate for unconsciousness. Whatever was going to happen, I didn't want to know about it.

The snuffling stopped. Scratching began. The wolf was scratching my tent with its paw. Not one wolf. At least two. Maybe three or four. I sat in the very center of my tent, as if, were one to claw through the fabric, it would only reach in a single paw, not tear the tent down. I cursed other campers who had kept food in their tents, who had taught these wolves that people meant a meal.

Then I started shouting. At the top of my lungs I told the wolves to leave me alone. To get away from my tent. To just go, just go.

I didn't faint, but I may as well have. Somehow I went back to sleep. When I awoke early in the morning, I lay in my tent wondering if I had dreamed the whole incident. Really now—wolves scratching at my tent. Perhaps not dreamed it, but certainly imagined it. Sounds on tents are often magnified. A scratching tree branch can send my imagination on a very long journey. But there were no tree branches here on the beach at the foot of McBride Glacier. Perhaps wind whipping sand against the fabric? This was Alaska, the animals were still wild. Certainly no wolves had pawed my tent in the night.

At not quite six in the morning I emerged from my tent and stretched. The air was fragile and tinged with the color of coral. Yesterday afternoon the icebergs in the bay had jostled noisily in their progress toward the mouth and out to sea, but now they slipped silently. I looked across the sand some thirty yards to the nearest tent, Georgena's. She was standing quietly outside her tent, too, and I sheepishly wondered if she'd heard my shouting in the night.

I stretched some more. Stood quietly some more. Looked around. Then saw him. A spindly-legged, very black wolf standing on the beach a good thirty yards away in the opposite direction from

Georgena's tent. He paused, momentarily motionless, ears at alert, and then trotted down the beach.

I shout-whispered to Georgena and pointed frantically, not wanting her to miss the wolf. She shook her head and looked at me oddly.

A moment later, the wolf was gone.

"Georgena!" I cried. "Didn't you see that wolf? There was a wolf standing right there on the beach!"

Again, she looked confused. She glanced at the area around my tent. Then she realized that I hadn't known. She told me that she had watched me emerge from the front end of my tent. As I did so, the black wolf had been standing at the back end of my tent, not six feet away from me. Georgena saw me stretch and look around. It didn't occur to her that I hadn't seen my wolf companion. In fact, the incident only increased her marvel at how comfortable I was in the wild. She figured I had seen the wolf and continued to stretch and yawn as if I had often breakfasted with wolves. Eventually the wolf padded to the other side of my tent and down to the beach where I then spied him.

I almost didn't believe Georgena's story. Until I inspected the sandy area around my tent where I found a virtual stampede of wolf tracks, as if a pack of them had circled my tent for half the night. Probably though it had been just the one lone wolf, the black wolf, who had made many laps around my tent, snuffling, pawing the fabric, being perfectly capable of shredding it, but not doing so. The one lone black wolf who for whatever reason was very comfortable out here, very comfortable with me.

Winter Den

The bear mother enters the earth before snowfall and dreams herself through winter, emerging in the spring with young by her side. She not only survives the barren months, she gives birth. She is the caretaker of the unseen world.

Terry Tempest Williams, "Undressing the Bear" in
An Unspoken Hunger: Stories from the Field

Great steaming piles of bright purple scat on the trail reminded me daily that the huckleberries, thimbleberries, and salmonberries were gloriously ripe and plentiful and that the bears were hungry. Katie and I also stuffed ourselves on the berries along the trail, rejoicing in the fresh fruit on this twelve-day trip of otherwise freeze-dried fare. Most years I hike in the Rockies as late in the autumn as possible, when the air is cold and hard blue, when I can awaken to a light snowfall that melts away with the first morning sun. The animals are tucking in, hunting their last meals, and the tourists are gone. The bears, if they've been lucky that summer, are fat and ready to turn in to their dens for the winter. Montana is particularly radiant in the late autumn, with its wet and molding mat of leaves underfoot, the hot white stands of birch, the fiery aspens trembling in the wind. The air smells of roots, cones, and soil.

This year we were traveling in an area densely populated with not just bears, but grizzly bears. I knew they were about to den, that they had only a few more weeks for adding fat to their winter flesh, and that we were trespassing in their habitat, were perhaps interfering with their end-of-the-year preparations. Yet I felt uneasy about the rangers' prescription for avoiding confrontations with the grizzlies, which was to make lots of noise while hiking. On the long drive over the Sierras, across the desert, and into the Rockies, Katie and I had joked about the bear avoidance techniques we could use. Our favorite idea was to carry CD players and to seat miniature speakers in the side pockets of our backpacks, blasting Aretha as we hiked. Surely the bears would prefer the diva's voice to ours, and I knew the grizzlies could use a little more R-E-S-P-E-C-T. We couldn't quite imagine carrying out the suggested methods of talking loudly, dangling bells, or shaking rock-filled cans while hiking through their pristine and lyrical homeland. So instead we tried to remember to call out when we were in particularly dense vegetation, as we rounded bends in the trail, or when we found fresh scat. But otherwise we did our best to not disturb ourselves or the other creatures enjoying, or simply surviving, the quickening autumn.

Visiting grizzly habitat requires a certain amount of grit. Years earlier, I had tried to camp in the tundra north of the mountain known to the native Athabascan people as Denali and later renamed Mount McKinley. I wasn't keen on encountering the Alaskan grizzlies, known there simply as brown bear, but I had hoped that the glory of the mountain would compensate for my fear. I rode the bus out the park road and when I arrived at a space—and space is the only word to describe the tundra of Alaska—that included a sky-filling view of Denali, I asked the driver to let me off. I stood by the side of the gravel road, my backpack on the ground at my feet, watching the bus disappear around the bend. I felt so tiny in that landscape, its scale so phenomenally grand, that it was as if I were in danger of being swallowed. If the sky were to take in one small breath, I would be gone.

In truth, the tundra was far more likely to swallow me than the sky. I stepped off the road into the slurpy stuff and tried to pick a destination. Except for the dazzling mountain to my east, there were no landmarks to aim for, just miles and miles of wide open tundra. I should have chosen to hike on one of the park's sandbars or ridges, but I had wanted the real thing, tundra, and tundra was what I got. That and grizzly bears. No sooner had I started slogging through the thawed meadow than I saw tracks. Dinner-plate-sized tracks and finger-thick gashes made by curling claws.

In retrospect I think that the space spooked me more than the bears. After all, out there it would be virtually impossible to surprise or scare a bear into attacking and they don't usually attack without a reason. What frightened me was the absence of trees to lean against or hide behind, the lack of a clear destination, not to mention the fact that I couldn't figure out where I would sleep in the squishy tundra. Wherever I lay down for the night, sucked into the earth, open to the biggest sky I had ever seen, I knew I would feel like a banquet laid out for all comers. And I just couldn't get over the size of those tracks. So after only a few minutes of walking, I mushed back to the road where I caught the last bus of the day returning to the campground.

Fear. The topic of *courage* in the wilderness has been so over-explored it's a cliché, but when fear is discussed it's seen only as a hurdle to vault over. I see it instead as a rich muck, a source. The Inuit people have dozens of words for snow, and it seems to me that we need as many for fear. There's the slow creeping fear that precedes a mugging, the adrenaline-pulsing fear that accompanies a harrowing climb, the blunt stab of fear when a seemingly safe situation turns unsafe quickly. The form of fear I hate the most is the sluggish, disease-like fear that has resided in me for years, like a fever that blooms and withers but never completely disappears. I have found myself stopping on city streets to touch the wall of a building, for support, to breathe, as this flush of fear courses through me. There is no apparent foe—if there were maybe I could grapple it into submission.

I believe this kind of fear builds, like mud filling a lake, over many years. Perhaps each layer of fear slushes into a person from a different source, and can maybe be identified, but the overall effect is a gradually rising bottom of sludge and a gradually diminishing body of clear water. A person does not realize she has *become* fear until it is too late.

It is this pervasive, angst-type fear that has sent me into the wilderness time and again. In the far wild, I can get closer to the bone of the fear, see it naked. By inhabiting mountaintops, deserts, the shores of winter lakes, I don't overcome the fear, I don't slip across some invisible line into courage, but I do get to sleep with the fear against my skin. Over the years, my fear and I have become intimate.

By the time I returned to grizzly country, this time Montana, my relationship to fear had evolved. My lifelong feeling of being untethered, my nomadic soul's need for aurora guides, had diminished as I came to better understand my animal self in relation to the mountaintops and mountain lions, the motion of the ocean and the musical humpbacks. I had begun to know, in the marrow of my bones, my place in the planet's ecosystem.

And so this time I entered grizzly habitat cautiously but willingly, and soon was distracted by the many other residents, including a perfectly camouflaged herd of bighorn sheep with their gracefully curving horns grazing on a hillside, an enormous bull moose with a rack the size of a small tree posing near a cold, reedy lake, and one particularly skilled mountain goat scaling the side of a bare cliff, up and down, up and down, not grazing, just showing off. I looked for mountain lions or their tracks. It rained, it snowed, we hiked, on and off trail.

After a particularly long, wet storm, Katie and I climbed the trail out of a deep valley, following Swiftcurrent Creek and its glacial lakes, rising quickly above treeline on our way to a high pass through the mountains. Extensive switchbacks scarred the hillside above the lakes and trees and we made our way up the long ramps until, after turning the sharp corner of one switchback, we faced, smack in the trail some twenty yards ahead, a large, cinnamon-colored grizzly bear.

Following the griz down the trail, with a camera plastered like an appendage to his face, was a day hiker who apparently had not taken in the National Park's omnipresent messages about not approaching bears. As the man neared the grizzly in pursuit of his photo, he drove the bear down the trail—toward Katie and me.

Knowing that the guy with the camera was clueless, and that the bear was not likely to give up the trail, our only recourse was to leave the trail and scramble up the steep hillside. With our heavy packs and the thicket of huckleberry bushes covering the slope, this proved quite difficult. I hoped that the bear would take the path of least resistance and simply move on down the trail.

But she didn't. She decided to follow us. I looked over my shoulder, breathing hard from the effort of scaling the hillside, and saw the grizzly leap from the trail onto the hill and begin to run in our direction. As I watched her approach, I prepared to drop to a fetal position, to cover the back of my neck and pray.

What I truly felt, though, facing this cinnamon grizzly, an actual predator, was a sense of relief. My experience in the Alaskan tundra was frightening because the bears weren't actually present, but their tracks spoke to the larger fear residing inside me. A specific threat is so much less scary than fear itself. Here, then, was the real thing.

As it turned out, that particular grizzly bear was not interested in me or Katie. She simply wanted to eat her huckleberries in peace, and we were in her way. The bear ran right past us, not even glancing our way, vaulting with astonishing grace for an animal of her size and bulk over the bushes that we had negotiated so clumsily. Her muscles flowed like waves as she bounded uphill, not stopping until she crested the ridge and disappeared on the other side. I hoped she knew of other equally bountiful berry patches where she could eat in peace.

That bears eat berries at all intrigues me. How does such a big animal subsist on such small meals? Cougars kill animals as large as themselves and feast on them for several days, but bears excavate little ground squirrels, dig roots, and pick berries. They must work very hard to fill their bellies. People too subsist on many small meals and we can become desperate in our efforts to obtain those meals. For that matter, we become desperate in our desire for all kinds of nourishment. I wonder if the bear feels as desperate as we do, and if not, why not? That grizzly bear eating huckleberries in Montana didn't appear desperate. What I remember best about her is her grace as she bounded up the hillside toward the pass. I was struck by the two meanings of the word grace: one is about movement, the other about a state of being. What does it mean to live gracefully, rather than desperately, in one's habitat?

In "Undressing the Bear" Terry Tempest Williams suggests using the bear as a kind of guide. "The bear," she writes, "becomes our mentor." So I began investigating Alaskan brown bears, learning how they construct elaborate caves for the winter. First they dig entrances about two feet in diameter, and then a tunnel that can be anywhere from five to twelve feet long, slanted slightly upward, a detail that allows cold air, but not warm air, to escape. The chamber is usually about four feet by three, and the grizzly lines it with dry vegetation to make a nest. Here she sleeps during the winter months.

Here she not only survives the harsh winter wilderness, but she gives birth.

A few months after my hike in Montana, all the bears there, including the huckleberry-eating bear who charged past us near Swiftcurrent Pass, had settled into their winter dens. I too wanted to build a winter den.

So one afternoon in California's Desolation Wilderness, I picked a good hillside with deep snow. Like the Alaskan grizzly, I dug a two-foot-wide entrance and a tunnel sloping upward so that the cold air could flow out and the warm air would remain in the chamber. Digging the chamber at the end of the tunnel was hard work. A bear's wide paws with sharp claws probably work much better at digging in a small cramped space than long, thin human arms wielding a thinner, equally long snow shovel. But I managed, and finally the cave was big enough. I punched a couple of air vents in the three-foot-thick roof with a ski pole so that my warm body wouldn't melt the cave from the inside. Finally, I shaved the top into a dome, smoothing it as much as possible to prevent dripping.

Instead of dry vegetation, my nest was made of a space blanket, a sleeping pad, and a mummy bag. After cooking and eating dinner outside the cave, I crawled in and turned off my headlamp. I liked the hard, cold walls of ice on every side of me. They shut out all light, so that the cave was absolutely black, and also all exterior sound, so that my breathing was like wind rushing down a canyon. I had expected to feel afraid, but instead I felt the complete absence of fear, not even a vestige of the native panic I have always known. I was calm and sure. I had returned to, even created, the magical ice cave in which I had been "lost" as a child. What else might the mentor bear show me?

I sat up and lit the candle on the ledge I had carved in the wall at my feet. Light leapt up the ice, and the cave glowed blue. As the candle flared and flickered, great shadows swelled and receded on the cave ceiling. I liked the bit of light as much as I had liked the black darkness. Soon even my breathing quieted and the silence was so profound my body and mind stilled to a state of grace.

The Breath of Seals

I feel terrifically fragile, a pile of bones held together by juicy cells, inside the Air Force LC-130, a menacing aircraft manned by lean men in camouflage suits. The camouflage is for the jungle, a mottled green and tan pattern, and I wonder why the military wouldn't wear white when deploying to Antarctica. The inside of the plane looks like a multifaceted torture chamber with a tangle of pipes overhead, complicated and mysterious hardware covering every surface, and webbed sling seats for the passengers. The women's "bathroom" is a rustic toilet set up on an unstable crate only partially enclosed by a rough curtain. A student of mine told me that these LC-130s, also known as "Hercs," were the exact kind of airplane he flew in Vietnam.

This environment is difficult to square with my mission to Antarctica. I'll be the artist-in-residence, a guest of the National Science Foundation. My task is to create something. Yet I am encapsulated in a military plane designed for destruction. The load master, the guy in charge of cargo, which includes me, hands over earplugs and a sack lunch, then motions toward a red, webbed seat. I fasten myself in and open the sack lunch. The two fat sandwiches, apple and banana, juice and water, cookies, candy bars, chips, and even condiments for the sandwich are comforting.

The pilot starts the plane's engines.

I put in the earplugs, wondering if I have finally gone too far in pursuit of a high. Whatever happened to backpack trips in the Cascades where a mere field of wildflowers back-dropped by a glaciered mountain sent me over the top? Or even, long before that, my elusive fairyland? I have held a memory my whole life, although by now it's probably just a memory of a memory, of a moment in my early childhood. I stood alone in what may have been just a bunch of tall weeds. I only know they were taller than me and that their greenness, their bursting seeds of possibility dispersing airborne fluffs, enveloped me in magic. A true fairyland.

That feeling from a time when tall weeds held unbearable beauty has put me on this combat plane headed for the coldest, windiest, and driest continent on Earth. Somehow this crazy mix—of fairyland, combat plane, and Antarctica—makes sense to me, folding together all the parts of the evolution of my relationship to wilderness. Over the years, life bashed up against my weedy fairyland, that perfect synchronicity of imagination and wildness, until one day I couldn't find it anymore. In fact, I became unsure whether the fairyland actually existed geographically or lived solely in my imagination. It didn't really matter because the fairyland had launched my quest for all things wild and imaginary. From the magic ice cave of the Mount Jefferson Wilderness to the disenchantment of that blizzardy weekend in Hope Valley. From feeling stalked by deer hunters with guns to stalking mountain lions with binoculars myself. Then abandoning the tense predator/prey relationship altogether in my desire to understand the cougarness of cougars, the whaleness of whales, the bearness of bears. And now, sitting in this bullet of steel being prepared to hurl through space, there is just me, the humanness of me. I am well on my way home.

I settle back in the webbed seat and brace myself for takeoff. The noise of the engine is overwhelming. I don't feel the plane begin to roll down the runway. I don't feel it lift off the ground. I only realize we have taken off when I see clouds speeding by the window. It is the smoothest takeoff I have ever experienced.

It hits me: I am flying to Antarctica. It seems a miracle when I think that only a couple of hundred years ago Captain James Cook wrote in his journal, "The greatest part of this Southern continent (supposing there is one), must lie within the polar circle, where the sea is so pestered with ice, that the land is thereby inaccessible. The risk one runs in exploring a coast, in these unknown and icy seas, is so very great, that I can be bold enough to say that no man will ever venture farther than I have done; and that the lands which may lie to the South will never be explored."

It is an awesome moment to realize that I will accomplish, if that word is appropriate given my air force escort, something Captain Cook did not.

Soon after the perfect takeoff, the load master motions that I may undo my seat belt. I unbuckle myself and stumble to one of the small windows. Below me is the forty-fifth parallel and the last bit of the south island of New Zealand. Before me, the Southern Ocean, the roughest water in the world. Beyond that, the continent of Antarctica where, at a minute's notice, a storm can obliterate all visibility. If we reach the Ice, as Antarctica is known by the people who work there, in a blizzard, we will be in serious trouble. The pilot will not be able to land the plane safely, and we will not have enough fuel to return to New Zealand. That is why, when we get halfway there, the pilot will radio ahead to find out what the weather is like. If it's clear, we'll go on in. If it's bad, even questionable, we'll return to New Zealand. A third of all flights headed for Antarctica are forced to turn around midway. This is called the point of no return.

I press my face against the porthole and my tears steam the window. I spent my childhood making walks to the grocery store into treks in the jungle, the hill climb to my best friend's house a first ascent of a South American peak. This, however, isn't imaginary. I am being transported—deployed, as the National Science Foundation and air force put it—to Antarctica. With a mission. With an honest to god mission. To write stories.

For hours I stare out the window, watching the transformation of the sea as we move south. First a glassy sheen hints at the threshold of freezing. Soon patches of pancake ice, opaque disks with lacy edges, bob on the ocean surface. Finally they connect to form a sheet of frozen ice. The sun, just off the plane's wing, is bright and bursting with every color of the rainbow.

The load master invites me into the cockpit. When I climb up into the cramped space, I'm amazed to find one of the three crew members asleep. I glance out the cockpit window, as if I had been mistaken about the frozen sea and daggers of sunlight. We are long past the point of no return, and our prospects look fine. Still, I had expected my deployment to feel more like the sound of the word, a severely regimented journey. I'm given headphones with which I can listen to the crew's conversation, or join in if I choose, but I'm afraid to even breathe into the small mouthpiece. I had expected tense concentration from the pilot, but he's discussing his schedule for the rest of the week, and then last night's dinner.

A crew member motions that I am free to scoot around the cockpit. The pilot moves his coffee mug so I can squeeze myself into the small space beside him to be closer to the window. Mountains loom into view. My first sight of the continent. The snow is so pure it glows lavender and the air so clear the mountains look close enough to touch. Yet we fly and fly and fly, never quite arriving.

"Where's Mount Erebus?" the pilot asks, leaning forward, squinting at the horizon.

"Should be here somewhere," the copilot answers, scanning the landscape of mountains and ice.

We have begun our descent. I strain my eyes, looking for the active volcano that shares Ross Island with Mount Terror and the American base, McMurdo Station. I have read accounts of planes careening onto the ice runway, pilots blinded by the snow-choked air. Anything can happen weatherwise in Antarctica. But today the air is so clear and ethereal, the only danger I can imagine is looking right through anything so corporal as a mountain to its essence.

Still. I expect my pilots to recognize Mount Erebus.

They're chuckling now. A little joke, a little let's pretend we're lost for the daffy writer. I will learn, soon enough, that in Antarctica artists and writers are considered at best charming dreamers, society's clowns. A job someone has to do, but thank god, most workers in Antarctica think, it doesn't have to be me.

I'm prepared for disembarking, my first step on the continent. It's too big a moment to invest with much fanfare, so I deplane casually. And I am shocked, in spite of my planned flippancy, by the jolt of joy that transfers from the ice right up through my boots. If I didn't have to behave for my air force escorts, if I wasn't so aware of being a corny writer, I would kiss the ice. I really would.

This is *my* point of no return.

I am sent directly to survival school where I will camp on the Ross Ice Shelf, a permanent glacier that has flowed right off the continent and over the surface of the sea. The ice is six hundred meters thick, and I know I'm not in danger of falling through, but just the idea of the black sea sloshing below my feet is daunting. Ross Island is really just two big mountains, Mount Erebus and Mount Terror, and if my gaze travels up the glacier on which I'm standing to the top of Mount Erebus, I see a large plume of smoke curling from its caldera. I'm told that the mountain is the most active it has been in fifteen years and is spewing volcanic bombs. Though I can't see the bombs from this distance, the plume swirls and swells with impressive force.

133

Shelter is my first assignment at survival school. I pair up with Patrick who tells me right away that just before leaving for the Ice he met a woman who loves motorcycles as much as he does and he regrets having come. I can barely look at him while he speaks, so little do I relate to his regret. I am feeling no ambivalence. I sink my shovel into the snow and begin digging our snow cave.

The beauty of snow shelters is that they are very warm. Snow is always thirty-two degrees above zero, and so a snow cave is at least that warm. In a tight, well-constructed one, a person's body heat can warm it up much more. Here in Antarctica the temperature can drop to fifty below zero. Knowing how to build a quick snow shelter can save your life. The fastest shelter to construct is a trench covered with blocks of snow.

Our trench quickly becomes a luxury model, particularly when we learn that Donna would like to join us. First we dig a long deep trench with steps leading down one end of it. Next we cut two body-sized shelves, sleeping platforms, into each side of the trench. For Donna we dig out the back end of the trench, enough room for the bottom half of her body. The top half will occupy the hallway, or trench floor, of our shelter. Finally we use a saw to cut huge blocks of snow that we transport on sleds—some crumble and must be replaced—to the two sides of the trench where we tip them against one another, forming an arched roof. We pack snow in all the cracks.

As we build, Patrick, Donna, and I check out the shelters of the other students attending survival school, all new arrivals to the Ice. Some shelters appear much more elegant than ours, and others more crude. A large group is working together to build an igloo. They throw all their gear in a huge pile. Then they shovel an enormous amount of snow on top of the gear. They pack the mound of snow hard with the backs of their shovels and then by stomping on it. When the igloo walls are thick enough, they dig a passageway into the gear and pull it out, piece by piece. They will sleep in the cavity left by the removed gear. It's not a bad method, and it's fairly quick, but I much prefer my den with its cathedral ceilings and three semi-private berths.

Together the survival school students build a wind break of snow blocks for our kitchen, and then we fire up the stoves. We're instructed to eat two entire freeze-dried dinners to provide our bodies with enough fuel to heat us through the night. Getting down this freeze-dried feast is the hardest part of survival school. Anticipating the night, not wanting to be cold, I manage to do it with only a couple bouts of gagging.

Finally it's time for bed. I lay out my Therm-a-Rest pad and the warmest sleeping bag made, supplemented by a thick fleece liner. Wearing expedition-weight long underwear, a full-body heavy-duty fleece suit, a fleece jacket, and two hats, I get into my cupboard. This is accomplished by slithering feet first down the hole until I am lying on the floor of the trench. Since there is not enough room to sit up, I must then roll from the floor up into the unzipped sleeping bag on my shelf. Quickly zipping up my bag, I expect to be overcome with claustrophobia, the ceiling of ice just inches from my face, but I am surprisingly relaxed. The trench roof glows with a comforting blue light. I'm nearly warm. I actually fall asleep.

Some time in the night I awaken and crawl outside to look around. The sun never sets in the summertime here, but the light is dreamy. A mysteriously beautiful fog is swirling on top of the ice, so that as I ski away from camp I can't see my own feet. It looks like Sunday school pictures of heaven. The two mountains seem to float in and out of the clouds, and I'm drawn toward them, away from my snow shelter, that familiar urge to explore, maybe just as far as that small ridge over there. I keep glancing over my shoulder to make sure I don't lose sight of camp. Then suddenly I chicken out, remembering where I am and that the tiniest miscalculation of judgment

135

could doom me. I ski back to camp, descend into my ice home, and roll into bed.

Soon I am once again asleep inside a glacier of Antarctica.

The following day our instructor puts us through simulations of a number of wilderness emergency situations. The class ends with a contest in which groups of four people have to set up a winter tent with three deadman anchors (deeply buried snow stakes that won't pull out in eighty-knot winds), light a stove for boiling water, set up the radio (including a fifty-foot long antenna), and call McMurdo for help. My group accomplishes these tasks in just five minutes and forty-one seconds, setting the record for the entire season of survival school.

Sleeping in the snow on purpose at survival school is one thing. Pretending to be stranded in the wilderness and forced to live by my wits has been my lifelong favorite game. Having to do so in an actual emergency, however, is quite another thing. The whole time I'm in Antarctica, that possibility remains in the forefront of my thoughts.

On Christmas Eve I board another LC-130. As the only passenger, along with a big load of cargo, I fly with the air force crew into the interior of Antarctica to deliver supplies to two remote camps. Four people live and work in Byrd Camp, named for Admiral Richard E. Byrd, the first person to fly over the South Pole. Our second stop will be Siple Dome, a much bigger camp where ice core studies reveal climatic secrets of the planet.

As we land at Byrd Camp, I hear the pilot say that the weather is "going down." There is discussion as to whether I will be allowed to deplane at all because the pilot is in a hurry to make it to Siple Dome before the storm gets worse, but the load master tells me I may get out briefly. As the crew shoves a pallet of cargo out the back of the airplane, I step into the storm. The air is thick with furiously blowing snow, nearly obscuring the silver plane a few yards away. Not far off I see a few blotches of color through the blizzard, the tents of Byrd Camp, and from that direction emerge the four inhabitants. A woman hugs me fiercely, having no idea who I am but ecstatic to see another human being on Christmas Eve. She shouts, "Welcome," in my ear, and I have to say, "What?" a few times to hear her over the storm and the plane's engine.

The air force crew, who are all wearing Santa hats, get hugs too. I look again in the direction of the blotches of color that were the Byrd Camp tents and can no longer see them. For the four workers here in the interior, this weather is more common than anything else. Their jubilation is brilliant against the backdrop of white and makes me intensely aware of my humanness. There are subzero temperatures, a blizzard, a steel airplane, and this unlikely grouping of people. We cling.

Then I am directed back to the plane. The four folks left behind scurry over to the pallet lying in the snow, their supplies for who knows how long and their Christmas mail. I wonder how they will drag it to their camp. There isn't time for us to help. Our weather window is closing fast.

The pilot sets the LC-130 on its course down the "runway." Tries to, anyway. The skis on the bottom of the airplane stick in the newly fallen snow. He guns the engine over and over again, but the plane barely budges. Some crew members jump out and make adjustments to the skis. It works and we are able to slide forward. With greater and greater speed, we ski along the snowy ice, in the middle of the continent of Antarctica. I wonder if we are going to ski all the way back to McMurdo. Then I understand that the pilot is trying to take off but can't get the nose of the plane to lift. He tries again and again, as the engine makes an awful grinding noise. Finally he tries a faster approach. We get a good head of steam on and the plane lifts off the ground. Then it gently falls back down again.

I think: Here I am, in the middle of a blizzard in the heart of Antarctica, in a plane that can't take off, and the conditions are worsening. It is a very white, very close to the bone, truth.

We will either wait out the storm here at Byrd Camp, sharing their bit of shelter and eating into their supplies for however long a storm in the interior of Antarctica blows, or we will fly away in this storm. I wonder which I prefer.

The load master shouts in my ear, "We're going to have to shift the weight, push all the cargo to the back of the plane. If that doesn't work, we may need to strap you back there as well. The front is too heavy for liftoff."

He wasn't joking. A vivid picture of myself strapped onto a great pallet of cargo in the back of an air force combat plane springs into my mind. Camping out a few nights at Byrd Camp is looking better.

The big hatch at the back of the plane is opened. The men heft, shove, and adjust the load, and the plane is closed up again. We all buckle our seat belts, and the pilot roars off down the makeshift runway another time. The plane's nose lifts and we rise. And keep rising. We have become airborne.

I had looked forward to using the facilities at Byrd Camp, but our aborted visit prevented that from happening. I don't find the women's facilities where I had found them on my last Herc, and the men's urinal is not female-friendly, so I finally ask the load master if he can set up the women's toilet. He says that the cargo is in the way and he can't. I vow to never leave McMurdo again without my pee bottle and funnel. If I had them now I could use them behind a pallet.

Bodily functions are discussed openly in Antarctica. When survival is at stake, being delicate about human waste is a waste of time. When I first arrived I was issued a pee bottle and funnel. Antarctica is the most pristine continent and the scientists working here hope to keep it that way so their work can be as devoid of human contamination as possible. People carry clearly marked urine bottles.

Women also carry funnels, but the funnel issued to me was broken. When I tried to exchange it I learned they were out of them. The woman in charge of issuing gear told me that homemade ones have "better coverage" anyway and directed me to the carpenter's shop to get an empty container of a specific kind of solvent. The man in the shop found me one, washed it out well, and gave me scissors along with advice about making a good spout. His suggestions were good and my pee funnel does work very well. When I have it with me.

I'm soon distracted when I hear the pilot announce, "I don't think we're going to make it."

I know how to build a snow cave. But if the airplane crashes, will I live to do it?

Nothing happens. The plane doesn't plunge to the ice. The crew moves about the plane, calmly taking care of business and talking about their plans in McMurdo tonight. I eventually realize that the pilot only meant that we aren't going to make it to Siple Dome. A couple hours later we land safely at Williams Airfield near McMurdo Station.

Airplanes do occasionally crash in Antarctica. A couple of days after my adventures in the interior, I ski with some friends out to see one such plane that had crashed in 1970. The wreck still lies out on the permanent ice field.

The day is glorious and at thirty-six degrees above zero it's downright hot for Antarctica. Mount Erebus looms above us as we ski, a plume of smoke curling luxuriously from its hot caldera. My companions and I decide that the weather presents a photo opportunity too great to pass up: We strip down to nothing but boots, skis, and poles, and then take turns snapping pictures, front and rear views, of ourselves skiing naked in Antarctica. I am not thinking about survival.

Until we reach the downed plane. Only a wing, its tail, and the long spine remain above the ice, glistening metallic against the hard cold snow. I climb up on the tail and walk along the top of the plane, exhilarated at being alive, at skiing—even naked a couple of hours ago—in Antarctica. The crashed plane is like a grace note in this landscape, a ring of clarity about just how vulnerable we are in such aching beauty.

On the return ski, I see my first set of penguin tracks, a waddling pair of webbed feet with a trailing tail mark in the center. Since we are miles from the sea, I wonder what this one lone bird is doing so far from its colony. After following the set of tracks for quite some time, I come to an intersection of tracks, where another lone penguin has crossed paths with the first. The tracks cross at right angles and both sets continue on for miles in straight lines. It's extraordinary, this great X in the snow, like some kind of message. I see no birds, no other tracks at all, only this intersection of two lone penguins traveling far from home.

I've grown quite tired by the time we are offered a ride. A big orange Delta, a truck with giant tires (three feet wide and a five foot radius) made for the snow and ice roads of polar regions, has come to see if we are okay. Joe, the driver, is a fireman in New York City most months of the year. He is also a fireman here in Antarctica.

We are in fine spirits and climb high up on top of the Delta's cab rather than into the back of the vehicle. We sing and tell jokes as Joe drives us back toward Williams Airfield. The truck lurches. The top of the cab tilts and I feel myself sliding toward the edge, a good fifteen feet above the snow-packed road. I brace my rubber boots on the cab roof. The Delta comes to a stop and luckily so do I. Joe jumps out of the driver's seat and explains that he has accidentally slipped off the road into deeper snow. It's no problem, he says, but maybe we had better jump off.

We do. Joe works on getting the Delta out of the snow bank, but the more he guns the engine, the deeper the big fat tire spins into the snow.

We have radios and several of us confer, deciding we should call for help. Joe, however, is insistent that he can get the Delta out of the ditch. I slowly come to understand that he is mortified: the people we would call for help are his coworkers at the firehouse. They would never let him hear the end of having driven off the road. So we give Joe a little more time, watching him spin the tires of the Delta, digging a deeper and deeper hole in the side of the road. We take turns shoveling out the stuck tire, hoping to make a passage for it to move forward. When we aren't digging, we wait. And grow cold, in spite of the warm-for-Antarctica weather. It is getting late. I'm tired and hungry. I change into my spare socks to warm my feet and walk away from the Delta and then back, many times, trying to warm up. But I grow colder. And colder and colder. I look out across the vast field of ice and think of survival.

I do know how to build a snow cave. My pack is stuffed with survival gear, including extra clothing and food. But I would much rather sleep in the bed assigned to me in McMurdo Station. The rest of my skiing friends agree, so we take matters into our own hands and call the fire station. Minutes later, a fire truck races out the snow road. Joe's colleagues are hanging out the windows of the fire truck, laughing, snapping pictures of his misfortune, and shouting jokes that he will hear the entire season, and probably next season, too. Even the ambulance roars out the road to deliver covered plates of dinner for us stranded skiers who will miss galley hours in McMurdo.

The Delta is towed out of the ditch it made, and we are transported back to town. As I bounce along in the Delta, this time *inside* the vehicle, I savor the idea of a warm bed rather than an ice shelf in a snow cave.

I love McMurdo Station. My whole life I've longed to live in a frontier town—as a child, I read every pioneer diary I could find—and finally here I am. Like most frontier towns, McMurdo is desperately ugly. The buildings are brown boxes, the hillsides are churned, and piles of ugly crates and seemingly random machinery litter the outskirts. Most workers in McMurdo rarely if ever get out of the town and the place hums with pent-up energy, released by humor, music, and sometimes violence. One night a couple of guys get into a fist fight over cards because someone has insulted a woman. McMurdo really is a frontier town.

Just beyond this knot of humanity is stunning wilderness. From the window in my office in Crary Lab, I gaze across the sea ice to the Royal Society Range, and later, when the ice melts, I watch whales dancing just yards away. Sometimes I sit in my office for the containment it offers, much like a tent gives rest from the raw openness of wilderness. I can never stay indoors long, though, and am drawn outside over and over again, searching out each destination with a curiosity more pure than I have ever felt.

On many days I climb Observation Hill, which is right on the edge of town. At the top is a big cross in memory of Scott, Wilson, Oates, Bowers, and Evans. A plaque lists their names and says, "who died on their return from the Pole, March 1912." Then it quotes Scott's motto (the last line from Tennyson's "Ulysses"): "To strive, to seek, to find, and not to yield."

Each time I read this line I am jolted by its trajectory, an arrow of rigid purpose. Not to yield? That man had a serious attitude problem. He has raised the question, for all explorers, of the nature of exploration. If the goal, or the thing sought, is fixed, unalterable, is discovery even possible?

One night four of the youngest workers in McMurdo decided to go for a hike. The group of friends, two girls and two guys, set out following a safe, flagged route. They were having a good time, laughing, talking, watching the colors of endless light shift over the surface of the snow. The night was beautiful. But after a while they became tired. It was getting late, and they had to be at work early in the morning. They decided to take a shortcut. They left the flagged route to walk across a big field of snow where they would meet up with another flagged route.

Halfway across the shortcut, one of the young women dropped from sight. Literally. She had fallen into a crevasse that had been hidden by a layer of snow. As the girl felt herself falling, she had no idea how far she would fall or where she would land. She pressed her back against one side of the crevasse wall and pushed her feet against the other, managing to stop her fall.

Her friends peered down into the crevasse and found her that way, braced between the two walls of ice. Luckily, they had brought a radio. They called back to the fire station in McMurdo for help, and a few minutes later, a search and rescue team arrived. Using ropes, they hauled the girl out of the crevasse.

Her muscles were exhausted from holding herself up and she was quite hypothermic. Another few minutes in that crevasse and she probably would have died.

I hear the whole story one night at a town meeting in McMurdo. It is hard to listen to because the four young people are so scared—both by what had happened to them and also of speaking about it to the community.

"The hardest part," says one of the young men, "was when we were waiting for the search and rescue team. We didn't know if they would make it in time. We stood at the top of the crevasse. She was really cold. She was really tired. She didn't know if she could con-tinue to brace herself between the walls of ice." Now the boy's voice cracks with tears as he says, "She asked us to tell her family how much she loved them, and also how sorry she was."

There are rumors that these young people have been forced to tell their story to the McMurdo community as a punishment, but they say that they have chosen to speak publicly on their own. They have been badly scared. They want other people to know that one step off the trail, one broken rule, can be life-threatening in Antarctica.

I know that, and I also understand their misstep. The intensity of the beauty here overwhelms the fear, and I venture out time and again. On New Years Eve I ski to Castle Rock with two friends. When we begin at 9 p.m. the sky is an ethereal blue, powdery and soft, and the mountains and snow fields are creamy white. We reach Castle Rock shortly before midnight, leave our skis at the base, and climb the huge reddish outcropping. As we near the top, a lovely, eerie sound drifts through the icy air waves. On the summit I find a young man who works for search and rescue playing a didgeridoo he has made of plastic tubing. He serenades in the new millennium.

We sit on the top of the rock for as long as we can stand the cold. Between one and three in the morning there is a hint of a sunset with a tinge of pink and yellow in the sky. A few amazingly beautiful clouds to the west and some layered horizontal ones in front of Erebus cast lovely shadows on the mountain's glaciers. I can't dream of a more perfect way to celebrate the new millennium than skiing in Antarctica. I am overwhelmed with gratitude to be here in this most beautiful of all wildernesses on Earth.

A few days later, when Brian Stewart, a New Zealand scientist, invites me to help him count Weddell seals, I enthusiastically accept. Early one morning we ride in a tractor-like polar vehicle several miles away from McMurdo to the edge of the continent, near a place called Hutton Cliffs.

To reach the sea ice we have to climb over the pressure ridges, great blocks of ice crunched up against the continent. Even though the surface of the ocean is frozen, the tides still move the water up and down the shorelines, causing the ice to buckle and separate, creating these big jumbles. It takes a minute to find a passable route through the pressure ridges, but Brian has been here many times before and leads the way.

Once on the sea ice, I strap on crampons and we set out in search of Weddell seals. Unlike the permanent ice field where I attended survival school, the sea ice will melt out later in the season. For now it is still mostly frozen and slick as a skating rink. Brian gives me a long pole to prod the ice ahead of me as I walk. There is the chance of weak spots and cracks. He carries a rope, too, just in case someone misses a weak place with the prod and falls through the ice into the frigid sea. I think of how I wear a wetsuit when sea kayaking in the San Francisco Bay because even there the water can be cold enough to induce hypothermia after just a few minutes of exposure. Here in the Ross Sea, would I even have time to grab Brian's rope?

A moment later, I'm up to my knee in a crack. Sea water surges around my leg and a jolt of adrenaline sends a danger message throughout my body. It's a small crack and I extract my leg without help. I have on high rubber boots, so my feet aren't even wet, but I am all too aware that it could have been a much bigger crack, that I could be swimming in the icy Antarctic waters, flailing for the rope I hope Brian would have tossed. One step off the flagged route, one moment of inattention, one forgotten piece of gear. It is not "man against nature." There is no contest. The only way to survive is total submission to this continent's demands. What could Scott have been thinking in his vow not to yield?

I slow down and jab my pole out in front of every step. The weather is beautiful once again, and once again, Mount Erebus graces the icescape with its enormous presence. After walking for about an hour, I spot a black, slug-shaped creature lying on the ice. She is fat and sleek, with gray spots on her hide, and she watches us languorously with thickly lashed bedroom eyes. She's as comfortable on the sea ice as I would be under a palm tree in Tahiti. We approach cautiously, and Brian gives me a pair of binoculars. He tagged a number of the seals last year, and now he wants to see if the same seals have come back to this location and which ones have new pups.

Though we are able to get very close to the seal, we do not touch her. Using the binoculars, I read the number off the tag on her tail and Brian records it.

We continue on toward Hutton Cliffs where we find lots of seals, many with pups, scattered all over the ice. When we come upon a small hole in the ice, I stare in awe. To think I am actually seeing a seal's breathing hole, not five feet away. All around me, Weddell seals loaf on the sea ice, but I realize that this is only half of their world. Much of the time they are swimming under the ice. Brian tells me that he has camped out here on the sea ice, and at night as he lies in his tent he can hear the seals swimming and vocalizing, right below his bed.

As I marvel at this breathing hole, the tiny portal between the seals' two worlds, up pops a seal. She takes a breath of fresh Antarctic air and flops herself out of the hole and onto the ice. Brian tells me that most Weddell seals eventually die of starvation because their teeth wear out carving breathing holes. Once their teeth are gone, they can't catch food and they simply die.

Earlier in the year, Brian watched a seal die another way. He had been approaching a mother and her pup, hoping to read the number on the adult's tag. As he drew close, he heard a loud groan. Looking up, he saw the enormous blocks of ice forming the pressure ridge above him shift. In a flash, he realized that the blocks of ice were crumbling. Brian leapt out of the way, just a moment before the great mass of ice crashed down, but the two seals were buried. Four minutes later, the mother seal had chewed her way out from under all the snow and ice, but she couldn't save her pup. Then she died, too, a couple of hours later, probably of internal injuries.

After counting dozens of seals, we stop for lunch next to a big pool of open water caused by the tidal separation of the pressure ridges. We eat sandwiches and energy bars while we watch one seal playing in the pool, diving, surfacing, diving again, watching us as happily as we watch her.

Heading back at the end of the day, I just can't get over that I am hiking on the sea ice in Antarctica. Though I am tired and my pack feels heavy, it's all so mystically beautiful. Mindful of the crushed seal mom and pup, I stay a good distance from the pressure ridges. I look out for cracks and weak places in the ice. I step carefully on the tips of my crampons so I won't fall. The day is ending, and though the sun will never set, it does dip lower in the sky. The flanks of Mount Erebus reflect rainbows of colors from the sunlight.

I stop briefly and wonder if there is a seal swimming beneath my feet this very moment. It's too cold to stop for long. What chutzpah to be here at all. Humans just aren't made for Antarctic survival. We have no fur and very little fat compared to seals. We're relatively poor swimmers, and we can't go for more than a few seconds without air. Really, compared to these seals, compared to so many other animals, we humans are poorly endowed for life *anywhere*. We get by on our wits, but our wits are so deeply flawed. For every brilliant solution we find, there's a matching bit of havoc we wreak. I wonder if we are just a passing species, a mere moment in the history of life on Earth.

Antarctica is the perfect place to study species adaptation—the opposite of not yielding—and a few days later I make the journey to Cape Royds to visit a colony of Adelie penguins who make their home here quite happily.

"I'm going to load you hot," the helicopter coordinator shouts into my ear. "That means that when the pilot touches down, he isn't going to shut off the engine. You'll run out to the chopper and climb in."

We are standing on the edge of the helicopter landing pad, near the sea ice, on the outskirts of McMurdo. A National Science Foundation chopper zips in over the ice, hovers for a moment, and then gracefully lands. I'm frankly terrified in any aircraft that seats fewer than twenty people.

"Let's go," the coordinator shouts and runs toward the helicopter in a crouched position to avoid decapitation by the rotary blades. I follow in the same manner, dressed in my extreme cold weather gear, referred to simply as ECW gear, and carrying my sleep kit.

When we reach the chopper, the helo coordinator shouts more instructions, telling me in which compartments to stow my bags, what handles to *never* touch, how to work this thingamajig so that the cargo doesn't unload over the sea ice, and how to fasten the complex seat belts. She races through instructions about the helmet with headphones and talking gizmos—if you're in the front seat and want to talk, you push something with your foot, if you're in the backseat, you press a button in a handheld thing, all after you've plugged yourself in, which requires finding the thing in which to plug in and where to plug it. She then gives me the thumbs up.

I manage to stow my gear in the cage hanging on the outside of the chopper, get in, and do my seatbelt. We lift off and the pilot banks the chopper so that I am nearly parallel to the sea ice, and for a moment I am sure I will lose my breakfast. And then . . . my fear flips into exhilaration. Below me a couple of seals lounge beside a crack, a quartet of penguins comically run and toboggan along the ice, and we are surrounded by drop-dead gorgeous mountains. I laugh out loud.

When we arrive at Cape Royds the weather is cooling and wind is kicking up. I will be camping in a tent for several nights, without the comforts of indoor plumbing and a galley serving hot meals. Michelle and Hannah, the seabird biologists who live and work at Cape Royds, sleep in bright yellow, tipi-style Scott tents but use a Polar Haven for cooking and data entry. The blue barrel structure is equipped with solar panels that provide sufficient energy for running their laptop computer. The camp's toilet is a bucket outside the

Polar Haven, which needs to be emptied occasionally into the big barrel behind the shelter. All human waste is flown back to the United States for disposal.

As soon as I arrive, I have to use the bucket, which sits in plain view of the Polar Haven's window. Once outside, I quickly realize that modesty is the least of my problems. The temperature is well below zero and I am wearing many layers, including a full fleece suit. In other words, I pretty much have to strip completely. I begin undressing, one layer at a time, only to watch the first layers take off in a gust of searing cold wind. I run after my clothes, find rocks to weight them to the ground, and manage to balance over the bucket. I feel as if I am in the first stages of hypothermia by the time I go back inside the Polar Haven.

I don't get to stay inside for long, though. Hannah and Michelle have work to do and my arrival has already delayed them. The morning starts with counting penguins.

We climb a hill and look down at the rocky cape—and at thousands of Adelie penguins hustling about the colony. Not only are the penguins very noisy—cawing, moaning, belching, gurgling, and chirping—but they're terrifically smelly. Overhead, their worst predator, the skua, soars in search of opportunities, and the penguins all crane their necks upward in unison, watching the flight pattern of the hunting bird.

The skuas' nests surround the penguin colony, and as we walk through their territory they become agitated. I carefully watch where I step so I won't disturb the nests, but I inadvertently draw near to one from time to time, and when I do the attending skua flies in for the attack. Picture a very big bird with the curved beak of a meat-eater, long sharp talons, and a nice wide wingspan approaching your face at speed. I reason with myself, as the fierce bird approaches, that it will change course at the last moment. But reason doesn't work too well when dive-bombed by a furious mom with talons and a very sharp beak, and twice I fling myself to the ground, covering my head. As the skua veers off above me like a retreating fighter plane I sheepishly stand up and dust myself off. I'm relieved when we enter the penguin colony where the seabird population is far more friendly.

The adult penguins all sit on nests made of stone, some warming one or two eggs, others snuggling up with their newborn chicks, which are anywhere from tennis ball to basketball size and just as round. The bigger ones do not really fit under their parents' stomachs anymore, but most of them try. A couple of the biggest ones are just beginning to crèche, meaning that they are coming out from under their parents' bellies and wandering around a bit on their own. Unlike their parents who are formally trussed out in black and white tuxedos, the chicks have cozy coats of thick gray down and black heads.

The skuas continue to circle overhead. One swoops in close to a chick, and the adult penguin screams and flaps its wings hard. The biologists tell me that a sharp whap of a penguin wing can do a good amount of damage.

Beyond the cape, lines of penguins waddle out across the sea ice on their sixteen-mile hike to the open water to feed. When they come to small cracks in the ice, the penguins stop and lean over, looking into the water, probably inspecting for leopard seals, before hopping over the crack and continuing on their way. The mothers and fathers share the job of watching the chicks, so they take turns making this journey to forage. When the adults return from bingeing, the chicks stick their entire heads down the throats of their parents, who regurgitate some of the food for their young to eat.

The penguins work incessantly on improving their nests. They search for new stones, often stealing from neighbors, and carry the stones home on the tops of their feet. I watch one attempt to take a stone from a neighbor. The defending penguin turns away from its chick for a moment, squawking in protest, and gives the stone thief a brisk swat with its wing. In that instant of distraction, a bright-eyed skua swoops down, hovers for a split second, its talons dangling, and then snatches the chick. Off it flies, clutching its meal while the parent penguin watches helplessly.

Grieving for the penguin parent, I try to anchor myself with the bigger picture, how everyone's survival is dependent upon this intensely interconnected web of protecting young and getting meals. I scan the horizon for something to distract me, the lilting beauty of the mountains perhaps, or maybe the healthy trek of other penguins foraging, when my eye catches another set of creatures crossing the ice. Humans on skidoos.

A few minutes later, we meet Ted of the search and rescue team down on the sea ice where he straddles a snowmobile. The sea ice is beginning to deteriorate, so he and his crew are removing stakes that were placed to mark a formerly safe route. He asks if we would like to ride with them out to a wide crack in the ice that has opened up a few miles away. Hannah and Michelle hesitate because they have so much work to do. Yet the core of their work is studying the foraging habits of the Adelie penguins, and recently some of the penguins have been foraging at this large crack rather than waddling the sixteen miles to the edge of the sea ice. They decide that it would be useful to get a closer look at the new fishing grounds.

While they run up the hill to the Polar Haven to finish a couple of tasks, Ted, who is also McMurdo's most avid historian, reveals that he has a key to Sir Ernest Henry Shackleton's hut here at Cape Royds. After unlocking it, Ted guards me as closely as the skuas guard their nests, making sure I do not remove a single utensil from the revered explorer's hut, which has been perfectly preserved. Of course I wouldn't think of stealing anything, but Ted can't know that, so I tolerate his close proximity as I examine Shackleton's stuff. The reindeer sleeping bags are as disgusting as they sound in the explorers' journals, leathery on the outside with coarse fur on the inside.

I love Shackleton because, in spite of his enormous accomplishments, he knew that yielding was exactly what he must do, over and over again, in the wilderness. Just ninety-seven miles from his goal of being the first person to stand at the South Pole, he turned back because he didn't believe he and his men would make it home alive if they continued. That speaks of a grace almost unfathomable—to possess a desire as enormous as being the first person to the South Pole, to actually have the means to fulfill that desire, and *then,* and then to have the strength of will to retreat, to yield.

When Michelle and Hannah return, we climb onto the backs of skidoos like biker chicks and zip out across the deteriorating sea ice. We follow the line of penguins who are alternately speed-waddling and sliding on their bellies, heading north, until we arrive at the crack. It is about fifteen feet across and splits the sea ice for several miles. Adelie penguins swarm in the water and on the edges of the ice, diving in and jumping out, and most amazingly, doing a synchronized dance in which large groups of penguins gracefully arch out of the water like porpoises.

I sit right on the edge of the ice by the crack for a long, long time. What a grand life the Adelies have. The Royal Society Range to the east and north. Mount Erebus to the south. The sky that creamy Antarctic blue. Before me the lovely crack in the sea ice, revealing the cold steel-gray waters of the Ross Sea, in which the penguins are frolicking and fishing.

I learn from the seabird biologists that flying and diving are evolutionary tradeoffs. As penguins became more successful divers they lost their ability to fly. They don't have hollow bones like other birds, but instead they have special air sacs that work a bit like scuba tanks.

As I sit, penguins walk right up to me. The animals in Antarctica have not learned to fear humans and regard us with surprisingly little curiosity. I do not touch either the seals or the penguins, but I easily could, so unafraid they are. The day is magic and I feel greedy in my desire for this wilderness, this beauty, this ease between me and other species. It's what I want most of all.

I stay with Michelle and Hannah at Cape Royds for a week, trying to be as helpful as possible. Each morning and evening one of them climbs to the top of a hill to check on the locations and activities of several penguins who are wearing tiny radio transmitters. Late one night I accompany Michelle. She holds up a crude-looking antenna attached to the center of a hand-drawn compass on a wooden disk. Swinging the antenna around, she tries to pick up signals from the transmitting penguins. When she finds one, she uses the compass to record its location. She also notes the strength of the signal, which helps to determine how far away the bird is, and whether the signal is broken, which indicates that the bird is diving. Simultaneously, other researchers are doing the same thing at Cape Bird and at Inclusion Hill. Using triangulation, they can determine the birds' exact locations. I help by recording the data as Michelle listens for signals and takes the readings.

Sitting on the top of the hill, I get very cold. Far to the north, way beyond the crack in the ice we visited earlier, I can just make out the *Polar Star,* the Coast Guard icebreaker that carves a path through the sea ice each year. The watery path is then used by the *Green Wave,* a ship that brings all the supplies the Americans need in Antarctica for the coming year, including food and equipment and machinery. To the south, I watch the gap between White Island and Black Island fill with white, the color of storm. Michelle notices too and we work quickly, a little spooked. This space between the two islands is due south from our present location. When a storm reaches that gap, they say it will hit McMurdo in twenty minutes and Cape Royds in another twenty minutes after that. The sky soon roils in white, and we hurry back to camp. That evening the winds gust up to fifty knots, strong enough to knock me over, and the temperature drops to twenty below. My Scott tent is very noisy as the wind hammers its sides. I worry about the penguin chicks even though I know that unlike me they are perfectly adapted to this climate. Still, I'm sure they would rather not be blasted by frigid winds. Luckily, in spite of the storm brewing outside, I'm perfectly cozy.

In the morning, I awake to see that the storm has blown out all the sea ice north of the crack we visited earlier in the week. Fall is approaching. When the National Science Foundation helicopter comes to lift me off of Cape Royds, Michele and Hannah give me a packet of frozen penguin vomit that I am to deliver to the lab in McMurdo without letting it thaw.

After accomplishing this, I climb right back on another helicopter, nearly cocky now in my chopper *savoir faire*. Soon I am flying across McMurdo Sound, headed for the mountains, part of the Transantarctic range that snakes across the entire continent. Enormous glaciers slide down the mountain flanks. Wide valleys offer up frozen lakes. Strong winds from the south have swept these valleys free of snow and ice, giving them the name Dry Valleys, a misnomer really because this area is one of the few places in Antarctica where there *is* water, including lakes and the continent's largest river, the Onyx. Perhaps "Ice-Free Valleys" would be a more accurate name. While 98 percent of the continent is covered with ice, the Dry Valleys area is the largest ice-free region.

As we fly over a massive glacier on our approach into the valleys, the pilot points out a black C curved on the ice, my first mummy seal. Later I hike twelve miles alone in the Dry Valleys to see many more of these mysterious, dead sea mammals. Scientists believe that these mummified seals have been lying in their exact positions and locations for as long as three thousand years, perfectly preserved by Antarctica's dry and cold climate. Their bodies are very skinny, giving the impression that they starved to death, but why were they up in the Dry Valleys, many miles from the sea, in the first place? No one knows for sure. Another part of the mystery is that most of the mummy seals are Crabeater seals, not the Weddells found in the nearest sea.

Today we fly right over the ancient seals, and also over the frozen lakes of Taylor Valley—Fryxell, Hoare, and Bonney—on our way to Pivot Peak in the southern Dry Valleys. I'll be staying with a group of geologists who are studying glacial moraine in order to determine the history of global warming. My pilot has never been to this part of the mountains and is confused by the GPS reading. It tells him that we have found Pivot Peak and the high, broad glacier-carved basin beneath it, but we see no sign of a camp here. The GPS reading says we should be hovering directly over the tents. I look out the window of the helicopter and see nothing but peaks, glaciers, the one basin.

"Has to be here," the pilot says.

I begin to feel nervous as he rechecks his instruments. He shrugs and the helicopter plummets to that icy, windswept basin. As we draw closer to the ground, we are both amazed to see three bright yellow Scott tents, astonished at the scale of things here, how the massiveness of the landscape dwarfs anything human-sized.

The pilot sets the helicopter down gently on a rocky area and tells me to hop out. Apparently, I am to unload myself "hot." I hesitate, looking out the window. The three tents are here, all right, but I don't see a single human being.

I open the door anyway, grab my gear from the cage, and then run, crouching, a distance from the helicopter. The pilot lifts off the ground and swoops away over the mountains.

The following moment is the quietest one of my whole life. I stand, entirely by myself, in the Transantarctic Mountains. I'm not scared, exactly. More like deeply awed. One human life, after all, is utterly insignificant alone in these wildest of all mountains. I think of those mummified seals, stranded, far from their habitat. Not wanting to share their fate, I try to figure out what I should do next.

Shelter is always a good first bet, so I drag my gear toward one of the yellow tents. As I do so, I think I hear a tiny whinny.

I glance around. Certainly no birds live up here. There is not a single tree.

But there it is again. A tiny whistle.

Straining my eyes, I search all the ridges surrounding the camp. Finally, I see them. Four miniscule figures, looking like ants, on a ridge far above me. They are shouting and waving their arms, their voices barely audible. I realize that they want me to join them. I know right away that this is a test, so I change into a lighter jacket for climbing, pack a knapsack, and climb the ridge, keeping a steady pace. At the top I find Dave, the geologist, and his team, who immediately comment on my speed in climbing the mountain. I'm glad to be among humans again.

I spend the next two days digging pits in rock and then—after the geologists have taken samples, notes, and pictures of the exposed rock layers—filling in the pits. It's what I imagine prison work to be like. Backbreaking. I'm not very good at it. I can't shovel sediments and other rocks as well as I can climb a ridge. Sometimes I give up, painfully aware that I am succumbing to their definition of the soft artist/writer. Already Dave has told me that reading is for people with lots of leisure. He mocks botanists (flower sniffers) and entomologists (butterfly chasers), seeming to believe that geology is the only real man's science. Rocks, and nothing less. He prides himself on having a no-comforts camp. The three men brag about not washing their hands, and Dave claims to have gone for ninety-six days one year without changing his underwear. There is one young woman at the camp, Jane, who is twenty-two, and they tease her mercilessly. They call her Jimmy because a woman geologist is something they claim they cannot imagine. Jane is studying the volcanic ash in the Transantarctic Mountains, so they have penned "Jane's Ash" in big black letters on the back bottom of her jacket. I admire her perseverance, how she laughs along with them, but in a way that tells me she knows this job is just a means to an end, the career in geology she wants so badly.

The camp looks out over the enormous Ferrar Glacier, which has a wet-looking, glossy surface, completely smooth and unbroken by crevasses. One day we all hike to the lateral moraines directly adjacent to it and then scramble down into the deep gap between the moraine and the glacier. From there I stare up at the nearly vertical side of the glacier, a wall of ice two stories high. There is a place where the moraine has accumulated right up next to the river of ice, and after climbing this, we're able to walk out on top of the Ferrar Glacier. We chip off pieces of the ice and that night pour Scotch over them. As the shards of glacier melt in our drinks, air that has been trapped in ice pockets for thousands of years is released.

Breathing in the ancient air, I think that Antarctica is like a hallucinatory drug, a place where the intensity of beauty, feelings, and thoughts is felt to its full potential, is not obscured by the static of everyday life. It occurs to me that I am getting to spend three months just thinking about Earth itself, as if I am having an affair with the planet. This makes me acutely aware of my humanness. How all the striving I do, trying to stay on course, trying to figure out what my course is in the first place, is absurd. What is important in life is achingly clear here: that caring about living creatures, including other people, and our home the Earth is the most essentially human thing to do.

Flying back to McMurdo from Pivot Peak, I notice how much of the sea ice has melted in the week I've been gone. The entire surface is cracked, forming a mosaic pattern, and something is squirming in the cracks. I peer down from the chopper and glimpse shiny black and white hides. Orcas. Not *an* orca, not even a pod of orcas. The cracks in the ice are *full* of whales.

I shout my excitement into the headset, bringing on a sharp reprimand from the pilot, who doesn't appreciate the blast in his ears. Nevertheless, he descends and lands the helicopter on a piece of sea ice, next to one of the swarming cracks. For half an hour, we watch a group of five orcas playing and fishing. Occasionally one bobs vertically, upper body out of the water, to watch us too. Do they find us as stunning as we find them? What is the ecological aesthetic of a whale? I am often relieved to not be a scientist so that I am free to ponder these questions.

Upon my arrival back in McMurdo, I search out Commander Wheeler of the Coast Guard to learn the status of the *Polar Star.* Earlier in the season I had asked if I could be on his volunteer lines-handling crew. He had agreed and I attended the training, aware as usual of my suspect role as the artist-in-residence. At times I feel as if people allow me to think I am participating when all along they are covering my every move. Once I accidentally wander, with my camera perched prominently on my chest, into an off-limits zone in McMurdo. It's very cold and I've covered every inch of skin. Even so, I am approached within seconds of entering the off-limits zone by someone who knows who I am, identifies me by my full name, and escorts me out of there.

Still, I try very hard to overcome my greenhorn status and I intend to be an exemplary lines-handler. The day the *Polar Star* is spotted on the horizon, I receive a message to be on the lookout for the icebreaker's arrival in Winter Quarters Bay, the small harbor alongside McMurdo Station, some time in the next few days. I am to report to the ice pier as soon as I see the ship drawing near.

The ice pier at McMurdo Station is one of only two in the entire world, the other being in Siberia. During the winter, workers set up a big rectangular enclosure on top of the sea ice, and then they pump a layer of water into this oversized tray. After the layer of water freezes they pump in another layer. They keep adding layers of water, and letting them freeze, until there is one huge ice cube sitting on top of the sea ice. The ice pier is secured to the shore by ropes and deeply sunk columns. Finally, a layer of soil is spread on top of the ice pier for traction. During the summer when all the sea ice melts, the big ice cube remains floating. It is strong enough for ships to tie up to. It is also strong enough to hold container trucks that drive right out onto the ice pier to get loads of cargo from the ships.

The *Polar Star* can be seen for several days before it arrives. It proceeds slowly, having not only to cut through the thick sea ice, but also to travel back and forth in the path it has already cut to keep the ice from freezing over again. Like everyone in town, I'm excited about its imminent arrival.

Then an unfortunate thing happens. A storm far to the north sends giant sea swells that surge under the ice pier and crack it right in half.

I walk down to Hut Point, the small peninsula that wraps like an arm around Winter Quarters Bay, to see the damage for myself. The sea is still heaving under the ice, and the pier rises and falls, rises and falls, as water gushes up through the big crack that divides it in two pieces. In the distance, I see the *Polar Star* approaching.

Over the next couple of days, Commander Wheeler's crew works to mend the broken pier. First they try to pour water into the crack, hoping that it will freeze and thereby "glue" the two pieces together. This does not work. So they drive stakes into the ice on either side of the crack and then wind cable back and forth from one stake to another, stitching the crack right up. I return to the pier that evening to see the repair. Water still floods up through the crack. I can't quite believe it will be strong enough to endure the container truck traffic. There is really no choice, though. The *Green Wave,* which follows the *Polar Star* into port, must be unloaded. Otherwise, the station will be without supplies for the year.

I finally get the call that the *Polar Star* will arrive within twenty-four hours. As a lines-handler, I am requested to keep a sharp eye out all day. I check the horizon every few minutes, and the ship always appears to be a great distance away. I think I'm being vigilant, so I'm astonished when I look early in the evening and see that the vessel has already pulled up to the pier. I'm late.

I jump into my extreme cold weather gear and sprint down the long road to the ice pier, the entire route of my run in full view of the rest of the lines-handlers and Commander Wheeler. He stands on the pier at midship with his arms folded across his chest, mirrored aviator glasses hiding his eyes, looking every bit the commander. Not a word to me as I arrive late and panting and take my position on the pier with the crew at the stern of the ship. I feel like the exact artist-in-resident I've heard jokes about and been warned against being. There's nothing to do but try my best now that I have arrived.

Stepping out on that big floating ice cube—with a crack down the middle of it—is unnerving. Staring up at the *Polar Star* from the vantage of the ice pier is downright daunting. The vessel looks unnaturally huge and unwieldy. The lines that we will use to tie up the ship are bigger around than my arm. With a Coast Guard mate overseeing me and the rest of the crew at the stern, I stand on the pier and wait for the sailor onboard to pitch out the first line.

I try to remember everything that I've been told. I'm not to catch the rope ball at the end of the line. Doing so would badly hurt my hands. Instead, I am to hold my arms out straight so that the line will fall over my arms.

That part I do fine. After the line lands on the pier, my team pulls it as hard as we can, tug-of-war style, until we are able loop it over the cleat. The trick is to not let any of the line fall into the water. It does kiss the sea for a moment, but we keep hauling on the rope, and the mate in charge doesn't scold us. In fact, she commends us. A second line is thrown, and we catch it. This time the mate orders, "Now, dip the line."

I'm excited that I remember that "dip the line" means to slip it under the first line before putting it over the cleat. So I drag the big line, stepping over the first one, and start to "dip" it.

"No, Lucy, no," the mate barks at me. "Get away from there!"

I leap away from the line. Someone else grabs it and hooks it over the cleat.

I don't know what I have done wrong, but I don't have to wait long to find out.

She growls, "What if the ship had surged? That line you stepped over would have popped up. It could have sliced you in half. I've seen it happen."

Later, after the *Polar Star* is all tied up, the mate puts an arm around my shoulders and smiles. "Nice job, Lucy." She's kind, but of course I hadn't done a very nice job at all. In fact, people say, "No, Lucy, no!" so many times while I am in Antarctica that a friend who drives a bulldozer at Williams Airfield makes me a plaque that reads,

LUCY BLEDSOE

GUEST WRITER

MCMURDO, ANTARCTICA

"NO, LUCY, NO!"

Even so, I pass some kind of muster because I'm offered the Antarctic pièce de résistance: a trip to the South Pole. I had been told when planning my adventures on the Ice that a trip to the Pole was highly unlikely, and that if it did work out, I should expect to fly in and out on the same day. Bed space is extremely tight at the Amundsen-Scott South Pole Station. But I learn that I'll be staying for an entire week. Mysteries in Antarctica are limitless and I am learning, slowly, to ask fewer questions, to just accept.

My flight to the South Pole is delayed for hours, first due to problems with the aircraft's hydraulic system and then because of a problem with its skis. The LC-130 is finally okayed for flight, and we take off in yet more inscrutable Antarctic weather. We fly over the Beardmore Glacier, the mother of all glaciers, where scientist Ralph Harvey searches for meteorites and also where many of the great explorers climbed to the polar plateau. It's no wonder those fellows struggled, given the heavily crevassed surface. I'm grateful to Admiral Byrd for pioneering flight to the Pole.

When we land, the load master opens the door and I step out on the polar plateau. I expect to be met, but no one is here, so I follow one of the four other passengers who seems to know where he's going. He moves fast, too fast, and because I am dragging a big duffel, I can't keep up and soon am on my own. The South Pole is a huge construction site, the new station scheduled to be completed in a couple of years. The old station is a silver dome nearly buried in snow. I spot its bald top and head in that direction, finding a corrugated steel opening, a distance from the dome, but certainly leading there. I walk through a long tunnel lined with frosted pipes, castoff equipment, and confusing turnoffs to other underground passageways. I keep walking—briskly with my head up as if I'm in an unfamiliar cityscape and wish to appear completely at home—and eventually find myself inside the dome.

I had expected a toasty enclosure of small buildings but find instead a dim space, lit only by the natural light finding its way through the passageways. There is snow under my feet and the thickly frosted ceiling of the dome is decorated with hundreds of long icicles. None of the prefab temporary buildings are marked to identify what goes on behind the closed doors. I feel like I am in a science fiction story and must select one industrial freezer door to open. As I stand momentarily indecisive, a woman pops out of an orange door. She pegs me as a newcomer and without introduction suggests I rifle through the recycling bins for a chamber pot, explaining that my sleeping berth will be a long walk from the bathroom and it is many degrees below zero. The immediate practicality of these people can take your breath away. If I don't find an appropriate container, she tells me, find her in the galley. She disappears behind the orange door. I rifle, find nothing, and so enter the orange door, which happily turns out to be the entrance to the galley. She digs up an empty pickled ginger jar—"with a screw lid, even"—and gives it to me. I self-consciously shove the jar into my knapsack and look around the galley. I see that there is some dinner left, warming under heat lamps, and help myself.

Like in an airport, a broadcast system covers the entire South Pole Station. While eating my dinner I hear, "Lucy Jane Bledsoe, report to the galley. Lucy Jane Bledsoe, report to the galley." Fortunately I am exactly where I'm supposed to be. Eventually the station manager shows up for my in-brief, which consists of handing me a pamphlet about the station and telling me, "Just don't get into trouble."

I have been advised to go right to bed to avoid high-altitude sickness. Though it snows only a couple of centimeters each year, it is so cold and dry that the snow never melts, so that over millions of years the altitude of the South Pole has reached that of many peaks in the Rocky Mountains—nearly ten thousand feet—even though the terrain is perfectly flat. I'm used to being in high altitudes and feel wonderful from the second I step off the plane, but I head off in search of my bed anyway

On the way, halfway between the dome and the tent city where I've been assigned a bed, I find the geographic South Pole. The place is marked with a simple sign that must be moved ten meters every year to accommodate the shifting ice. Near the geographic South Pole is the ceremonial South Pole, marked by a striped barber pole topped with a mirror ball. The original signatory countries of the Antarctic Treaty—an agreement to keep the continent exclusively for peaceful purposes—fly their flags in a semicircle around the pole. The station workers are all busy at their jobs, and so I am completely alone at both the geographic and ceremonial South Poles. Though the Earth is spinning as it always does, while I stand in this spot on its axis, I don't spin with it.

The moment is exhausting and I head off once again for my bed, which is located in a temporary, barrel-shaped structure that accommodates about ten sleepers. My "room" is tiny but private, like a berth on a ship, with a curtain drawn around the bed, a bit of a desk, and a reading lamp. I lie down and try to digest my location on the planet. These musings are soon interrupted by a voice coming over the intercom to announce that all unnecessary uses of power should be turned off—lights, computers, anything that isn't absolutely essential. Pole Station is maxed out this year, bursting beyond capacity, because of all the people working on the construction, and it's not unusual for the station to run on its emergency power system.

The next day I explore the dome, climbing several flights of rickety stairs to the Sky Lab, a makeshift music studio in a glass room at the top of a tower. I look out the window, expecting a Rapunzel view, but because the snow has piled so high around the dome, the surface of the snow is quite nearby. Disconcerted and slightly claustrophobic, I descend to the floor of the dome again and search for the gym, impossible to imagine in this small space. Some of the passageways under the dome are off-limits, but I'm not sure which ones. I find a door to what I suspect is the gym and open it. The room is dark so I feel around on the wall next to the door and try a couple of switches. A light comes on. Bingo: the "gym." The tiny room has a wooden floor, a basketball hoop, and some rolled up yoga mats. I imagine some worker obsessively perfecting his or her jump shot over the course of a South Pole winter, and then I shut off the light and saunter back to the galley.

Just as I arrive, a siren sears the cold dim stillness. A man plows out of the galley door and shoves me aside, saying, "Move." People stream out of all the buildings under the dome and head for the tunnel leading to open air. Over the intercom a voice announces, "Fire in the gym, fire in the gym."

Had I inadvertently flipped a fire alarm? Could it be located right by the door, next to the light switch? I fall in with the groups of people leaving the dome, trying to decide if I should say something. But to whom? And when? Then an even worse thought occurs to me: Maybe there *is* a fire. The South Pole is a virtual desert and a fire would devour the station in minutes. This is not a place people want to be without shelter.

No one, however, is interested in talking to me at the moment, and so I leave the dome and retreat to my berth. No other announcements are made over the intercom and no mention is ever made of the incident. To this day I don't know if I triggered the alarm.

No place on the polar plateau intrigues me more than the Dark Sector, situated a half-kilometer away from the dome, where scientists are doing cosmology and other sensitive probing of the universe. It is of course never dark at the South Pole in the summertime. "Dark" refers to quiet, as in no noise or radiation interference.

One night I walk to the Dark Sector and meet Nils Halverson, who is working on the DASI (Degree Angular Scale Interferometer) telescope, which is in the final stages of construction. He takes me up a ladder through the innards of the telescope to the roof of the building, which serves as a throne for the receivers of the grand instrument. DASI looks completely different from other telescopes I have seen. A support structure of blue steel legs holds up yellow panels that look like petals surrounding the main body of the telescope, a big, shiny steel box that glints in the nighttime sun. On the face of the box, tipped toward the sky, are thirteen cylindrical receivers poised to look deep into the universe. The telescope is like a cosmic flower facing the stars.

DASI detects cosmic background radiation, ancient light coming from a time when the universe was very young, about three hundred thousand years old. In other words, the microwave telescope allows cosmologists to observe light that has been traveling since the infancy of the fifteen-billion-year-old universe. At that time the universe was much hotter—as in a couple of thousand degrees centigrade—and brighter, as well as much denser and much more uniform. It didn't have structures, such as stars and galaxies. The gases were just beginning to condense, or "clump." The cosmologists look for slight variations of the microwave light, the equivalent of looking for slight temperature fluctuations. These variations and fluctuations indicate when matter first started clumping. The cosmologists hope the data from DASI will allow them to measure the curvature of the universe and discover its mass and density. Then they will be able to determine if the universe is going to expand forever or begin contracting. Until recently, cosmology has been primarily a theoretical science studying the origin and evolution of the universe. DASI, and other telescopes like it, have begun to give cosmology the data it needs to become an observational science.

My timing is phenomenal. The cosmologists expect the new telescope, which they have spent years building, to receive "first light"— meaning it will be ready to operate—within the next day or two. Despite the auspicious moment in his career, Nils is not only generous with his time but particularly good at explaining cosmology to a layperson with clarity and contagious passion. For the next twelve hours, I return again and again to the building that houses DASI, hoping to be present for first light.

The next day I find the scientists drinking beer and cheering at their computer screens. First light. The telescope works. I gaze at the monitor wondering if I am seeing the beginning of the universe but Nils tells me that for now they are looking only at the Sun. They're ecstatic, however, that the telescope works and will soon be collecting data about our universe.

This probing of the universe—as well as the work of other physicists who bore two-kilometer-deep holes in the ice in order to detect the passage of neutrinos—is without question the most exciting exploration happening at the South Pole. There are loads of people, however, who still view the bottom of the Earth from a twentieth-century perspective, as a place to pit themselves against the extreme landscape. One day I eat lunch with a group of Argentinians who are snowmobiling across the continent. Later in the week, a Russian expedition arrives in glacier buggies, dune buggies adapted to ice travel. The vehicles have balloon tires and are so lightweight they can be driven right over a line of human bodies, which the Russians demonstrate using volunteer workers from Pole Station. To celebrate their arrival at the Pole, the Russians launch a huge, rainbow-colored hot air balloon. As the balloon lifts off, one of its passengers sweeps up a young woman who works in the South Pole Station galley and takes her along on the two-kilometer flight.

The crew here at South Pole Station has a somewhat tense relationship with the handful of expeditions that come through each year. There are no spare beds and little extra food. Usually the United States Antarctic Program makes them stay in their own tents but does feed them. According to the Antarctic Treaty, no nation owns any part of the continent, so some people's proprietary attitudes are a bit controversial, and yet understandable because resources must be so carefully planned out and accounted for. A couple of years ago, several people sky-dived over the Pole. Their parachutes did not open and the workers here had to clean up the corpses.

Despite the stories I hear, despite the mind-bending galactic exploration to which I have been introduced, I find that I am not immune to the lure of the polar expedition tradition. What is it about a horizon that is so enthralling? I want to leave the station. I want to experience the polar plateau in intimate solitude. I'm told that there is a small hut, dubbed Hotel South Pole, a couple of kilometers away from the station. I borrow a pair of skis, fill a pack with survival gear and lots of food, and then report to the communications office at South Pole Station. They give me a radio and request that I radio them when I leave the station, when I arrive at Hotel South Pole, and when I leave the hut in the morning.

The temperature at the South Pole this evening is thirty degrees below zero Fahrenheit, without the wind. Counting wind chill—and I definitely am counting it—the temperature is *sixty* degrees below zero Fahrenheit. I wear goggles with a fleece neck gaiter pulled up to the bottom of them. My head and ears are covered with two fleece hats. I ski hard to generate heat.

I love skiing away from Amundsen-Scott South Pole Station. Once I gain some distance between me and the silver dome, I see what the South Pole really looks like. The wind has carved permanent waves in the ice, called sastrugi, making the snow look like a frozen sea. When the wind whisks the dusting of snow into the air, each of the tiny ice crystals glows with an entire rainbow of colors. This magic snow, found only at the South Pole, is called diamond dust. Even with the diamond dust sparkling the air, the sky is so clear and the snow so pristine that I can see as big of a forever as I can hold in my heart. I can actually see the curvature of the Earth.

I surf across the frozen sea on my skis, flying through the diamond dust, glancing now and then at South Pole Station disappearing behind me. I'm aware of the pack on my back, the weight of food and survival gear a comfort rather than burden, and continuously pat my front to check for the radio that I keep close to my body, inside all my sweaters and heavy down parka, so that its batteries do not drain.

A black speck appears on the horizon, Hotel South Pole, where I will spend a night by myself. I ski hard the rest of the way and soon arrive at the small plywood box, painted black to absorb the unending sunlight and finished off with a wrap of clear plastic. In spite of this effort to trap the solar heat, I expect the inside to be very cold, so I'm surprised when I pull open the door and am overwhelmed with warmth. The eight-foot-square room is furnished with a cot, a

Coleman stove on a small table, and a wooden chair. After putting on water for tea and laying my sleeping bag out on the cot, I switch on the radio.

"South Pole Station, South Pole Station, this is Lucy at Hotel South Pole."

No answer.

"South Pole Station, South Pole Station, this is Lucy at Hotel South Pole."

Still no answer.

I suit up again in sweaters, parka, neck gaiter, hats, and goggles, and step back outside the hut, into the sixty below air, thinking that the structure is interfering with reception. I need to be quick so that the batteries do not drain in the cold. I try again to reach the station. Nothing.

This is disconcerting. Certainly I came out here on the polar plateau with the intention of being alone. But I had believed that I was connected to South Pole Station by this radio. I had thought that if I got into trouble, I could always call for help. It seems that I have a defective radio.

I stand outside the hut for a few more moments. The sun will never set, but it hangs low in the sky, the light making the waves in the snow appear to ripple. The silence is sublime. This kind of cold, so extremely dry, jumps onto a body. I don't feel stabs of cold pain. Instead, my hands go instantly numb.

I return quickly to the warm hut and shut the door. I drink my tea and crawl into bed with an anthology about women adventuring into the wilderness alone. The sun streams in the window at the foot of the bed and I'm actually hot, too hot. I strip down to long underwear. I try several more times but never am able to reach South Pole Station by radio.

I read for hours and only drift off into a dream-heavy sleep at three in the morning. A couple of hours after that, a *swish, swish,*

swish sound enters my subconscious like a foley artist soundtrack, touching my heart more than my brain. I feel a shadow cross my bed and awake all at once to find, in the window at the foot of the cot, a man's face peering in at me. His head is lost under a wool hat and his face is masked by a bushy beard. I'm now aware that the *swishing* sound was his skis approaching. I jump out of my sleeping bag and pull on my layers of clothes, but by the time I step outside the hut the man is already skiing away, just a tiny figure in the distance. Later it occurs to me that, since I never successfully contacted the station upon my arrival at Hotel South Pole, he has been sent to make sure I'm okay.

I am very okay. I eat breakfast and prepare for the ski home. Home. What a word to use for the South Pole, and yet it fits for me. I ski away from the hut until it is only a tiny mark on the 360 degree horizon. Then I stand still, truly alone. Diamond dust swirls around my face. The sky is a velvety blue, attached by only a thin line to the snow. The silence is like a beast, so immense and overwhelming. I am brimming with gratefulness for getting to be here. I don't mean here, as in Antarctica, or even here as in the South Pole, but Here, as in at this specific time-space in the universe. I feel as if I have wanted to get here, be here, my whole life.

The summer is coming to an end in McMurdo. Upon my return, I ski in the Antarctic Marathon, choosing the half-marathon route and still coming in last. The results are published in the weekly paper and in spite of my standing, I am proud to be one of thirteen contestants. I help a friend bartend in the coffeehouse one night, accidentally ringing up three glasses of wine as three bottles of wine, a mistake that cannot be undone in the coffeehouse's cash register, so it looks as if my friend and I have absconded with a significant amount of cash at the end of the evening. "No, Lucy, no." I take a cruise on the *Polar Star* one day, cutting through the slushy path in the sea ice, and see lots of orca and minke whales, Adelie penguins,

Crabeater and Weddell seals, one lone Emperor penguin, and beyond the sea ice, massive luminously cerulean icebergs that are unspeakably beautiful.

When the *Green Wave* arrives in Winter Quarters Bay, the National Science Foundation deems it time for me to leave. The ship-offloading process is dangerous and consumes the energy of all the workers in town, who put in twelve-hour shifts. All sales of alcohol are suspended during this time. Unfortunately for the workers, the first real autumn storm hits as they begin offloading the ship. For me this means a happy delay of several days for my flight north.

On the night the storm clears, knowing I will fly home the next day, I walk to Hut Point and sit for as long as I can stay warm, watching the ever-present orcas and minkes. When it is time to move again, I follow the shore, walking past the water treatment plant and the helicopter pad. The sea is a mess of ice and open water now. Near the continent's edge there are pools of slush, angular chunks of ice, and the remaining large plates of sea ice. I keep walking until I'm at the base of Observation Hill. It's a lovely Antarctic evening, the sky a blue so otherworldly it might float away if it weren't for the remnant storm clouds anchoring it to the Earth. The mountains across the sound seem to take on a thousand different poses in the shifting light. As I stand looking at these mountains I begin to hear a deep rhythmic *whoosh*. For a second I suspect the wind, and then because of the regularity of the sound I decide it is some water action caused by the tides. But the sound is unmistakably alive. A deep breathing. I search all the cracks and pockets of open water near my feet, looking for the seal that has to be, by the sound of it, *right here*. I can practically feel the movement of air coming from the exhalations but cannot find a seal anywhere nearby.

I continue my walk around Observation Hill until McMurdo Station is no longer visible. I have come to a place where there are a dozen Weddell seals lounging next to a couple of cracks in the ice. I sit on the reddish earth near the base of the hill and listen to the exquisite silence. Then a skua screeches. As if the skua were a conductor lifting a baton, the seals begin to stir. One baaas like a sheep. Another chirps. A seal in the water blows bubbles. The seals continue to vocalize their Antarctic symphony—baaaing, chirping, snorting, huffing—until all at once they stop. But they have shattered my illusion of silence. Now I hear the sleeping seals, lying on their beds of ice, breathing sweetly, steadily, even loudly. One seal is actually snoring.

When I walk back toward McMurdo, I stop again at the place where I heard the first, invisible seal breathing. This time I see her. She wallows in a shallow pool just a few feet from shore, entirely submerged except for the black end of her nose. She breathes in total relaxation, a deep woofing.